CANALETTO

CANALETTO

Nicholas Ross

STUDIO EDITIONS
LONDON

To my mother and father Joan and Mark Ross

First published in Great Britain in 1993
by Studio Editions Ltd
Princess House, 50 Eastcastle Street
London W1N 7AP, England

ISBN 1-85170-828-6

Printed and bound in Hong Kong

Frontispiece: Pen and wash drawing of the lagoon to the north of Venice, *c.* 1742. There is a similar drawing of this scene at the Ashmolean Museum, Oxford, which is thought to come from the period when Canaletto took a sabbatical from painting his more typical scenes of Venice for Grand Tourists.
The Woodward Collection

INTRODUCTION

In 1780, at the age of twenty, the talented William Beckford arrived in Venice on an August evening and left in his diaries an evocative and telling insight into what lay before him:

I have no terms to describe the variety of pillars, of pediments, of mouldings, and cornices, some Grecian, others Saracenical, that adorn these edifices, of which the pencil of Canaletti conveys so perfect an idea as to render all verbal description superfluous . . .

The son of a rumbustious sugar tycoon, William Beckford had received a startling education. He had been instructed in architecture by William Chambers, architect of Somerset House, his drawing master had been Alexander Cozens and he had been given pianoforte lessons by the eight-year-old Mozart. Given the considerable ability of Beckford as a diarist, it is high praise indeed that he should have considered himself unable to surpass Canaletto when describing Venice. Canaletto left more than three hundred paintings, and about five hundred drawings and engravings; however very few letters survive, and he made no comments about himself or his fascinating surroundings. Indeed, much of Canaletto's career is pieced together from the lives of his major patrons, who were young aristocrats from England on the Grand Tour of Europe. It is therefore no coincidence that there are remarkably few pictures by Canaletto on public display in Venice, most of his work having left the city during his lifetime bound for the great houses of England. If Canaletto is enigmatic one should perhaps not be surprised, for he came from a strong silent city which was once known for its masked secrecy. In any pursuit of Canaletto the individual, we are left clutching at straws like Beckford's description of gondoliers 'catching the air'.

On 30 October 1697 Zuane Antonio Canale was christened at the church of San Lio in Venice. Zuane is the Venetian for Giovanni and Da Canale is the family name of the artist we commonly know as Canaletto. He is sometimes called Canals and at other times Canaletti, but this is generally by contemporary Englishmen or Frenchmen. Canaletto called himself Canal or used the diminutive 'etto' suffix as an endearing way of distinguishing himself from his artist father. He lived in the family property where his father and uncle both had apartments, while a shop, a storeroom, two attics and three other rooms were let at other times. Though it was not a palazzo, the income derived from such a freehold, centrally placed at the heart of the city, gave the Canal family reason to think of themselves as comfortably accommodated.

Canaletto has always been considered remarkable as a topographical painter, outstanding for the detailed depiction of his buildings, for the vivid light which illuminates his pictures and the tangible space he invites us to explore. There is, however, no story being depicted, nor intellectual point being made. Canaletto essentially paints what is before him and it is therefore vital to know something of his main subject, Venice. The Venetians call their city La Serenissima, 'the most serene one', as it lies in the calmer waters of a lagoon at the northern end of the Adriatic. As if married to the sea, the streets filled with water, Venice is a city which breaks the normal divide between land and sea. The area was first settled as a defensive site by the erstwhile inhabitants of the north Italian peninsula as they fled from the terror of the invading barbarian tribes.

Given the proximity of the sea and the strategic position of Venice between the Byzantine Empire in the eastern Mediterranean and the Alpine passes leading to northern Europe, Venice soon became pivotal in European trade. This, together with the lucrative monopoly for salt production, so essential for preserving food, enabled Venice to acquire immense wealth and great power. As a cosmopolitan trading city, with diverse interests, Venice had a taste and style that were tailored by a mixture of influences. With the variety of ogee arches and Gothic trefoils, with Romanesque carving and Classical capitals, with the tall, narrow arches of Islam and the drilled mouldings of Byzantium, no wonder Beckford ceded to Canaletto's ability to suffuse the fine details of his surroundings with a sense of grandeur.

Some of Canaletto's most famous pictures are of Piazza San Marco and the Doge's Palace, which was the administrative centre of the city, a trading empire and far-reaching land dominions. The area of San Marco was laid out in order to give visiting ambassadors the impression of enormous and ancient power that saw no hindrance or bounds. By the time of Canaletto, the Venetian Republic had reigned unassailed for almost a thousand years and would do so until Napoleon conquered the city in 1797. Surprisingly, the history of Venice is not one of great individuals and leaders but of a system founded on anonymity. A series of checks and balances made it almost impossible for a doge, the elected figurehead of the state, or members of the executive council, the Council of Ten, to construct a power-base. The Senate and the Consiglio Maggiore were groups made up from a nobility (in 1719 there were 1,700 male nobles recorded) designated by the inclusion of their family name in the ancient *Libro d'Oro* (Golden Book). The names therein had remained largely unaltered since the early fourteenth century, thus inoculating the system against change and forming an oligarchy rather than a republic. George Orwell could hardly have expressed the principle better in *1984*: 'The Party [in the case of Venice, the patrician classes in the Golden Book] is concerned not with perpetuating its blood but perpetuating itself. Who wields power is not important, provided that the hierarchical system remains always the same.'

Within the hierarchy of Venetian society, Canaletto's family came from a definable class of *cittadini originari* (citizens by origin). Such a status was significant in a cosmopolitan trading city with a strong sense of identity and a glorious history. The cittadini originari were placed just below the patrician class of nobility, which meant that they could take no direct part in the government of the city. The Canal family could, however, carry a coat of arms of a blue shield with a gold chevron. In an engraved form this is shown under a portrait of Canaletto (see page 7) and it is occasionally seen in pictures by way of a signature.

The Republic of Venice was the envy of many states, a seductive Utopia which appeared to be rich and peaceful, and whose seat of government, the Doge's Palace, with its open, agreeable arcades, was quite unlike the Palazzo Vecchio in Florence, which resembles a fortress. However, veiled in security, the Venetian government had a steely spine, secret police and a terrifying civic inquisition. For those families inside the Golden Book, marriage abroad, or into other classes within Venetian society, was not generally encouraged. In a similar effort to strengthen the core of Venetian society, only the youngest son of a noble family would marry in a sort of reverse primogeniture. Wealth was thus concentrated down one line of the family and, for example, we know from records that two-thirds of Venetian nobility were unmarried in the late sixteenth century. By ceding such commonplace liberties, the Venetians perpetuated the state and enabled it to provide a stable backdrop against which all could profit through trade. It was, after all,

Title page for the first edition of
'*Prospectus Magni Canalis Venetiarum*',
Engraved by Antonio Visentini after G.B. Piazzetta, before 1735.

the state which maintained a huge navy to patrol the eastern Mediterranean protecting shipping and trading colonies against piracy.

Visitors to Venice were rightly in awe of its wealth and age. The wisdom of the republic and its sage conduct of diplomacy was much admired, particularly because by the mid-seventeenth century the once virile muscle of Venice was beginning to sag. After the fall of Istanbul in 1453, the discovery of America in 1492, and the forging of new trade routes around Africa, the focus of world trade moved from the eastern Mediterranean, causing the slow but inevitable decline of Venice. The arrival of visitors could not have come at a better time, bringing important income which softened the landing of La Serenissima's fall and providing new markets for artists like Canaletto. Grand Tourists, as they were known, travelled to Italy learning European manners, French fencing, Parisian dancing and the epic lessons of Rome. Thus the young English nobleman completed his education, acquiring as he went that essential of social success, taste. As Venice declined, so Englishmen sought self-improvement, looking forward to an age of humanism and self-determination, as Milton so evocatively describes in the late seventeenth century: 'Methinks I see in my mind a noble and puissant nation rousing herself like a strong man after a sleep, and shaking her invincible locks. Methinks I see her as an Eagle mewing her mighty youth, and kindling her undazzled eyes in the full midday beam.'

Venetians were glad of their rich visitors and did much to encourage tourism. For example, Protestants could feel safe from religious persecution because the Venetians themselves had been excommunicated three times since 1500. Additionally, efforts were made to cut down the risk of plague, a constant threat in a major port with no independent water supply, by establishing quarantine islands for newcomers from suspicious places. Meanwhile there were many entertainments, most notably the Carnival, which elsewhere was a short period of indulgence before the abstinence of Lent, but which in Venice had become a prolonged celebration lasting from Christmas, or even early October, until Shrove Tuesday. There were hundreds of theatrical and musical events, boxing matches, juggling displays and stalls. The choirs of Venice were particularly famous and one of them, the Mendicanti, was glowingly described by Beckford as 'the mendicanti, one of the four conservatorios, which give the best musical education conceivable to nearly one hundred women'.

Bernardo Canal, Canaletto's father, was involved in the theatre industry, having inherited a family firm specializing in set design. Since the time of Pietro Aretino, the great sixteenth-century poet, Venice had developed a virile tradition for theatre that boomed in the seventeenth century mainly on account of Monteverdi, Cavalli and Cesti, who collectively transformed opera from a courtly pursuit into a popular entertainment. By 1700 Venice had seventeen theatres for opera alone, most of which were built and subsidized by wealthy patrician families like the Grimani, who built the Theatre of San Giovanni Crisostomo. Each theatre vied for ever more spectacular performances, which hinged not only on the music but also on the stage scenery. Novelty was at a premium and with three seasons, the first of which ran throughout the Carnival, the second at Ascensiontide and the last in the autumn, there was great demand for a good set designers. Stage sets became works of engineering as well as artistry, making the profession highly skilled and valued to the point that sometimes the set designer's name appeared on the programme for an opera, but not the name of the composer.

There were other less cultivated reasons why Grand Tourists arrived in Venice. As early as 1608, Thomas Croyartt had noted that there were twenty thousand courtesans in Venice, almost twenty per cent of the population. In 1749 Sir Thomas Nugent went further, noting that women were to be seen in the street 'with their breasts open, and their faces daubed with paint', while Beckford wrote more poetically of '. . . a great many ladies negligently dressed, hair falling very freely about, and with innumerable adventures in their eyes'. Other tourists wrote in comparable terms about the delights of Venetian women, of their beauty and their cultivation. This may partly have come about because of the limited opportunities for marriage within the patrician classes. If, as in the late sixteenth century, only a third of the men from the Golden Book married, then it follows that roughly two-thirds of the women whose families were in the same lauded book would be unmarried. These young women sought security from the unmarried two-thirds of the patrician men as well as from suitable visiting Grand Tourists. By the time of Canaletto the licentious life style in Venice had peaked and is perhaps best exemplified by the adventurous and energetic life of Giacomo Casanova, who conducted a torrid and much publicized affair with the abbess of the convent of San Zaccaria. Convents themselves were full of the unwanted progeny of such assignations, and orphanages were equally crowded with girls who were arranged into choirs or orchestras, as Beckford commented concerning the Mendicanti.

Such was the liberal tenor of Venetian life that Gregory XIII lost all influence, remarking that he was 'pope everywhere except in Venice'. Meanwhile William Beckford, who was in a position to see life from another angle, mused that restraint was 'perfectly out of the question'. At certain times in the year the city must have been crowded, slightly disorderly and very dirty. 'Venice is a stink pot charged with the very virus in hell', wrote Dr Warner, an English visitor. Similarly, Samuel Sharp wrote in 1767: 'The nasty fellows . . . let down their breeches wherever or in front of whomsoever they please; accordingly, all St Marks place, and many parts of that sumptuous building, the Doge's palace are dedicated to cloacina.' Throughout his career Canaletto did not in any way record the daily revelry of eighteenth-century Venice, whereas others, notably Pietro Longhi and occasionally Giovanni Battista Tiepolo, give us a more realistic impression of that extraordinary place. Canaletto did depict, on the other hand, a clear, clean and beautiful city which its long history perhaps demands, rather than an image of a fallen queen overripe with sumptuousness. Those pictures by him of actual events in the city are of official showpiece celebrations, such as the *The Bacino di San Marco on Ascension Day* and *The Doge Visiting the Church and Scuola di San Rocco* (pages 89 and 93). The success of Canaletto, particularly in his thirties, must in part be due to his ability to produce sanitized and charming views of Venice for well-travelled Englishmen.

Canaletto went to Rome with his father around 1719–20, to design the scenery for two Alessandro Scarlatti operas, *Tito Sempronio Gracco* and *Turno Aricino*, for the 1720 Carnival. This is the first we hear of Canaletto, already aged twenty-three, and it is fair to assume that he had been working under his father for at least seven years. The skills which he would undoubtedly have acquired were those of architectural painting, perspective painting and the ability to create an illusion of space.

P.A. Orlandi, an early biographer of Canaletto who published *Abecedario Pittorico* in Venice in 1753, notes some additional drawings that Canaletto made while at Rome, saying that with 'admirable taste' Canaletto 'drew the beautiful ruins . . . and that few from the ancient world and no contemporary artist could equal him in the art of copying nature, which he did with such perfection and truth'.

There is a pen-and-ink drawing (see page 10) of the arch of Septimius Severus that lies next to the church of Santi Luca e Martina in the Forum, right in the middle of Rome. It is part of a series of drawings which were later engraved. There is no absolute proof that these are the first independent drawings by Canaletto, but they were subsequently engraved and annotated as being by him after his death. Additionally, there is a painting of 1744 signed and dated by Canaletto in the Cincinnati Art Museum which depicts an almost identical topography. This drawing exhibits many characteristics of Canaletto's later work: for example, there is no attempt to dramatize the scene, there is no apparent narrative and those figures that there are seem to be incidental, serving only to break up the foreground.

Canaletto's name appears on the register for the year 1720 of the Collegio dei Pittori, the fraternity for painters, which seems to indicate that he had by then returned to Venice. His entry into the Collegio may hint at a change of direction in his career or at least a greater independence from his father. Another of Canaletto's biographers, A.M. Zanetti, describes Canaletto returning to Venice because he 'solemnly renounced' the theatre. Such a flamboyant description may well be the over-enthusiasm of a later biographer, but the parting of the ways between father and son might indeed have been dramatic. It is clear that the scale and magnificence of opera in Venice was diminishing at this time and that the focus of innovative opera had moved to Naples by the 1720s. The Canal firm's work in Rome could reflect their success and renown outside Venice or it could be symptomatic of a trade in terminal decline in the city. One is tempted to suggest that Canaletto moved into topographical painting because he saw no future in his father's business, while recognising another sector which presented little competition.

The Arch of Septimius Severus, Rome, *1719–20.*
Pen and ink with wash on paper, 15.2 × 22.8 cm
British Museum, London

There had been Venetian artists before Canaletto, Gentile Bellini and Vittore Carpaccio for example, who had painted detailed topographical views of Venice in the backgrounds of otherwise narrative subjects. In the eighteenth century there were also other cityscape painters, but this genre of painting was not so popular with artists, largely because it did not carry the academic kudos of religious painting, history painting or landscapes heavily scented with the musk of arcadia. Of Canaletto's contemporaries there were two Dutchmen, Jan van Heyden and Gaspar van Wittel (also known as Vanvitelli, he helped with the design of the Trevi Fountain in Rome), but the most important competition came from Luca Carlevaris, who died in 1730.

Carlevaris had been engraving and painting views of Venice for some time. In 1703 he published a collection of 104 engravings of views of the scuole (fraternities), churches and campi (squares) around Venice. Many pen-and-ink sketches also survive of the inhabitants of Venice on the street – anything from chestnut roasters to parading nobility. These figures subsequently appear in topographical paintings by Carlevaris. A famous example, painted around 1707, shows the arrival of the Earl of Manchester as

ambassador to Venice. To the right is the Doge's Palace, home of the figurehead of Venice and the centre of government. Beyond is the Marciana Library with its regular classical design and in the distance we see the entrance to the Grand Canal and the church of Santa Maria della Salute. A contrived dappling of highlights and deep shadow illuminates the social scene, while the vignettes of Venetian life in the foreground, which are set against some uninspired architectural painting, are the most interesting part of the picture. The Earl commissioned this painting and took it back to England, along with the decorative painter Giovanni Antonio Pellegrini.

Though it is generally assumed that Canaletto had returned to Venice some time in 1720, it is only from 1725 that correspondence survives which directly relates to any commissioned works. Four paintings in two pairs were commissioned by Stefano Conti, a wealthy merchant from Lucca, which lies seventy-eight kilometres north-west of Florence. Both Conti

Entry of the Earl of Manchester into the Doge's Palace,
by Luca Carlevaris, c. 1707.
Oil on canvas, 132 × 264 cm
Birmingham City Museum and Art Gallery

and his son, Giovanni Angelo, had visited Venice and it is probable that the views taken in the first pair, of the Rialto Bridge area, were from the building where Giovanni Angelo had stayed. For the second pair it is clear from the correspondence that Conti wanted the scenes from further up the Grand Canal where he had once stayed, next to the Casa Businello. Stefano Conti already had three views of Venice painted by Luca Carlevaris but these were probably of the San Marco area, because Carlevaris scarcely painted any other part of the city.

The surviving correspondence is between Stefano Conti and his agent in Venice, Alessandro Marchesini. The latter's role was to commission the work from the painter, come to terms about price and subject matter, supervise the progress towards a timely completion, pay for the finished work, and arrange for its passage through customs and eventual transport to Lucca. Marchesini convinced Conti that he should commission Canaletto, saying that everyone is 'inevitably amazed' by his work and that in it 'light shines out from the sun'.

The correspondence between these two men is unique in the field of Canaletto's work. From the many letters we can ascertain much about Canaletto's working method, the prices he charged and the names of those who owned pictures by him before 1725. Thus, we learn that there was a Canaletto hanging in the Palazzo Sagredo and that it had been seen by Giovanni Angelo Conti. Zaccaria Sagredo, the son of a doge and very old by this date, was perhaps the most significant patron of the arts in Venice, and it must have helped Canaletto considerably to have a painting in his palazzo. Marchesini also tells us that the ambassador to the Holy Roman Emperor had bought one of Canaletto's views at an exhibition of paintings held annually outside the Scuola di San Rocco and it seems likely that on hearing of the calibre of this patron, Conti increased his order from one to two pairs of paintings.

In September 1725, the views for the second pair of paintings were discussed in the correspondence. As mentioned above, Stefano Conti wanted views from further up the Grand Canal towards the Casa Businello, but Canaletto complained, saying that he could not secure a good viewpoint. We learn from Marchesini that Canaletto '*va sempre su loco, e forma tutto sul vero*' (he goes always on location, painting everything in truth). If this statement should conjure up the impression that Canaletto painted on site it is misleading, if not an actual lie. It would have been quite impractical for Canaletto to paint a canvas ninety centimetres high and almost one-and-a-half metres wide, with such precision, from a first-floor window over several months. There is no contemporary evidence that he worked in this manner, added to which the habit of *plein-air* painting was not established until the nineteenth century in France.

We get a better impression of Canaletto's working method from a wonderful preparatory drawing for the view of the Rialto Bridge from the north which is inscribed *Vedute del ponte di Rialto in Facza*. It is drawn in ink with some pencil underdrawing, the view having been taken from the first or perhaps second floor of a building. Canaletto has used more than one viewpoint in order to encompass the complete scene and to make a satisfactory composition. He also includes a building on the left-hand side in deep shadow to provide a contrast to those buildings in sunlight on the right, and to anchor one side of the picture. The drawing relates very well to the finished picture (page 51), including the boats on the canal, the ladder in the left foreground, the awnings, the eye-level point and the sun splash in the bottom right-hand corner where *sole* (sun) is marked on the drawing. It is quite feasible that Canaletto should have made such a drawing with rapid strokes of the pen, compiling as it were his own shorthand notes before working up the full-scale picture.

Also amongst the correspondence from September, there is some discussion about the difficulty Canaletto was having in obtaining the colour Prussian blue. He used this colour consistently and the delays he suffered may have been caused by its recent invention and the difficulty in securing a good supply. Analysis of his paintings has shown that in his early work he went to some lengths to prepare his canvases. The sky areas are underpainted in grey which gradually changes from dark to light across the canvas. Buildings, on the other hand, are underpainted in red-brown or yellow-brown, while the canal areas are again founded in shades of grey.

At first, Canaletto asked for thirty *zecchini* for each picture but Marchesini, who was also an artist, swiftly beat the price down by a third. Even though all

The Grand Canal: Rialto Bridge, *1725.*
Pen and ink on paper, 14.1 × 20.2 cm
Ashmolean Museum, Oxford

four paintings are very large, twenty zecchini was still a considerable sum, especially for topographical views, which commanded lower prices than religious pictures. It seems that at this early stage in Canaletto's solo career he did not underestimate his own talents. Conti, on the other hand, was determined to get value for money, demanding not only original views, but a signed description by the artist of each prospect and a receipt of payment.

Throughout the correspondence, which lasted from August 1725 to June 1726, Marchesini lied to, or at least misled, Conti about the progress of the pictures. He perhaps did so in order to placate an anxious patron or he was himself misled, which seems more plausible because on both occasions he was later to admit his errors to Stefano Conti. One is inclined to sympathize with Marchesini in his thankless task of mediating between an agitated Stefano Conti and an artist he described as '*un poco soffistico, e dilicato*', which, reading between the lines, means that Canaletto was difficult.

Finally, Marchesini triumphed and Conti received his pictures, three of which were entirely original, though

Santi Giovani e Paolo and the Scuola di San Marco, *1725.*
Oil on canvas, 81.5 × 136 cm
Private Collection

it is likely that a view of Santi Giovanni e Paolo had already been sold at the San Rocco market to the ambassador to the Holy Roman Emperor. As a coherent group, supported by their documentation, these four pictures are a milestone in Canaletto's early career. Conti, like so many collectors, expressed the wish that his pictures should not be split up by later generations. Unfortunately, perhaps inevitably, Conti's collection is not intact today, but his four prized Canaletto paintings remain together and it is appropriate that all four are illustrated here (see above and pages 51, 53 and 55).

Though the Conti pictures are the first documented works by Canaletto, it is fair to assume that he had already acquired a reputation, certainly one big enough for Marchesini to persuade Conti to commission him instead of Carlevaris. Knowing that Canaletto was engaged by Conti in 1725–6, we can place some pictures before that date on the basis of topographical evidence. The pictures in question fall into two groups, the Liechtenstein collection and a group of pictures known to have been owned at one stage by the Elector of Saxony. The Liechtenstein group is so called because the pictures have been recorded within the official collection of the Princes of Liechtenstein since 1806. Prior to that date the ownership of the pictures and their original patron remain a mystery, although there is speculation that they may have been within the private collection of this royal household before that date. All four pictures are remarkably large and have the same dimensions. A brief survey of Canaletto's work reveals that pictures of this size were usually reserved for the home market. One might tentatively suggest, therefore, that the Liechtenstein group was originally meant for the walls of a Venetian palace.

The subject matter of these four pictures leads one to the same conclusion. All four paintings show Venice hardly at its best, interesting but lacking the picture-postcard image and blue skies of Canaletto's work from the 1730s. One picture of particular interest (page 45) shows Piazza San Marco – 'the finest drawing-room in Europe', as Napoleon later called it – looking like a building site. The grey paving stones and geometric white marble patterning which the reader will come to recognize instantly are not to be seen. Instead the square is floored with a herring-bone brick design with parallel marble gutters which run from east to west. Significantly, in 1723 Andrea Tirali laid the geometric design we know today and almost in the middle of the picture one can clearly see that some of the first stones of the new design have been put in place, thus securing the precise date of this particular picture

Another in the series shows part of the Grand Canal looking east from the Campo San Vio towards the church of Santa Maria della Salute, the dome of which is shown partly shrouded in scaffolding. Work was known to have taken place there in 1719, which enables us to date this picture around that time. Given the dates *c.*1719 and *c.*1723 and assuming the Liechtenstein pictures were commissioned as a group, we can conclude that they are the earliest ones known to be by Canaletto.

The Liechtenstein pictures can also be grouped together on the basis of style and subject matter, for there is a strong element of squalor and decay in Canaletto's depiction of Venice. It is true that Piazza San Marco was fast becoming a building site, but it is surprising that so many of the awnings hanging from the building on the left of the San Marco picture are particularly shabby. Also within the group, a picture of the Rio dei Mendicanti looking south (page 47) is one of the most surprising of Canaletto's career. It is unusual for him to devote a large canvas to a real view which was of no particular importance. The Mendicanti, the large building on the left, was one of the four orphanages in Venice for girls which the reader may remember from William Beckford's comments earlier. It is not a startling building and is far from the beaten track well worn by the Grand Tourist. Albeit a laudable and important institution, it would seem odd to commission such a picture, unless it was of some specific interest to the patron, perhaps a Venetian patrician. Much of this painting is given over to miscellaneous scenes of Venetian life, including what appears to be thread being put out to dry at the top of a right-hand building and a gondola boatyard in the bottom right corner. Interesting and charming as this may be, however, it does not seem an especially splendid image for the tourist to take home.

Given over to depictions of the mundane aspects of real city life, Canaletto also painted Venice with swift brushstrokes, deep shadows and moody, stormy skies. Both the Liechtenstein and the Conti commissions are distinguished in this respect and, together with some topographical hints, are every inch early Canalettos.

The group of five pictures from the collections of the Electors of Saxony, now housed at Dresden, is not a set like the Liechtenstein pictures but a disparate collection. All that is known about their early provenance concerns the picture of Santi Giovanni e Paolo and the Scuola di San Marco (page 57). This picture is reputed to have been bought by the ambassador to the Holy Roman Emperor in 1725 from a well-known market held at the Scuola di San Rocco on 16 August, the celebratory day of San Rocco and the occasion of a ceremonial visit of the doge.

Our cloudy and imprecise knowledge of Canaletto's early career is much illuminated by his association with Owen McSwiney, an Irish maverick who forged a path for Canaletto towards England and the lucrative Grand Tourist picture market. McSwiney was an actor and impresario who, in 1706, leased the Queen's Theatre on the Haymarket from Sir John Vanbrugh. By 1711, however, he was bankrupt and, unable to meet his debts, he fled to the Continent, where he eked out an unsteady living by organizing singers for impresarios in London.

While in Italy, McSwiney befriended the young Lord March, who was conducting a Grand Tour with his tutor. March was the son of the second Duke of Richmond, who in turn was the illegitimate son of Charles II by a daughter of Breton nobility, Louise de Keroualle. It seems that the King could deny her nothing, making her the Duchess of Portsmouth and their three-year-old son the Duke of Richmond. So blessed with generosity, the Duke grew up and offered the hand of his eighteen-year-old son, Lord March, to the thirteen-year-old daughter of the Earl of Cadogan in settlement of a gambling debt. Immediately after his marriage, Lord March left for a Grand Tour which took several years. Shortly after his return to England he was entranced by a girl sitting nearby at the theatre and when he enquired after her name he was delighted to find that she was, in fact, his wife.

McSwiney and Lord March formed an association which lasted for many years, the remnants of which survive in the form of forty-eight letters. In one of these letters, dated 8 March 1722, McSwiney refers to a hare-brained scheme to devise a series of twenty-four paintings depicting the imaginary tombs of the great and the good of English history, particularly those concerned with the Glorious Revolution of 1688, during which the blood relation of Lord March, James II, was deposed from the throne. This conceit was ten years in the making, no doubt because the pictures themselves were enormous and three artists were to be employed on each. The letter of March 1722 mentions pictures of the tombs of Lord Somers (page 49) and Archbishop Tillotson, for which Canaletto painted the architecture, with Cimaroli painting the landscape and G.B. Piazzetta and J.B. Pittoni doing the figures.

These are extraodinary pictures when compared with the bulk of Canaletto's work. The concept behind them is both fanciful and theatrical, and it was perhaps Canaletto's previous association with the theatre that encouraged McSwiney to commission him. It is telling, however, that Canaletto worked on only two of the set of twenty-four inventions and that he did so very early in his solo career. At this time, as discussed above, the only other pictures we know that he was working on were the Liechtenstein group. If McSwiney had wanted Canaletto to do more perspectives for his scheme, he did not help his own cause when he did so much to advance the career of Canaletto by introducing him to English gentry and particularly Lord March, who in 1723 became the second Duke of Richmond.

In a letter dated 28 November 1727, McSwiney discusses the shipping of two views of the Grand Canal painted on copper, which are similar, he writes, to two further pictures for a Mr Southwell. The latter pictures remain unidentified, but the two for the second Duke are still at Goodwood. Another pair, one of which is illustrated in the plates (page 69), were commissioned for the Earl of Leicester. The pictures in all three pairs, which are the same size and painted on copper, seem to be the portable type which McSwiney was commissioning from Canaletto for the English market. If McSwiney's commercial mind had any influence at all, it may well have been to extract the bright, breezy, portable views of Venice from Canaletto which form a considerable contrast to the larger, thunderous and more dramatic views he had completed up to 1727.

In the same letter McSwiney expounds on the frustrations of securing commissioned work from an artist who is rapidly becoming popular and overworked, and less careful to please his patrons:

The pieces which Mr Southwell has, were done for me, and cost me 70 sequeens. The fellow is whimsical and vary's his prices every day: and he that has a mind to have any of his work, must not seem to fond of it, for he'l be ye worse treated for it, both in price and the painting too. He has more work than he can doe, in any reasonable time, and well: but by the assistance of a particular friend of his, I get once in two months a piece sketched out and a little time after finished by force of bribery.

Mr Southwell seems to have wanted the pictures too much, because McSwiney goes on to submit his bill to the Duke of Richmond, saying that a pair of pictures similar to those of Mr Southwell cost twenty-two sequeens each. McSwiney could of course have been trying to improve his standing with the Duke by suggesting that he was getting a better deal, but it seems more likely that Canaletto did vary his prices at will. His work was in great demand, and he may have been keen to play dealers at their own game while he could. Besides, McSwiney also mentions that a pastel portrait by Rosalba Carriera cost twenty-four sequeens, which in many respects is an equitable sum for this type of painting, suggesting that Canaletto was not taking outrageous liberties. Accepting that there is almost no real evidence about Canaletto's character, it seems possible that he was a quiet man, well aware of his status within Venetian society and probably rather haughty towards insistent and grasping foreigners. Visitors could, however, be forgiven for their agitations when they wanted a picture but had insufficient time to wait for its completion and had to leave their trust, hopes and deposits in the hands of agents. One can perhaps imagine the fraught atmosphere and lack of peace around Canaletto's studio in the little parish of San Lio.

By 27 September 1730, McSwiney's comments in a letter to another client, John Conduitt, show his patience to be spent and his rancour venomous:

I'm glad you have given ye commission to Mr Smith for yr pictures of Canaletto, & I hope you'l like 'em when they are done; I am, it may be, a little delicate in my choice, for of Twenty pieces i see of him, I don't like eighteen & I have several, sent to London yt I woul'd not give house room to, nor two pistols each. He's a covertous greedy fellow & because he's in reputation people are glad to get anything at his own price.

'Tis above three years yt he has Two copper plates in his hands, for ye D. of Richmond & I thought it wrong to sett him at work on a new work till he had delivered wt he has been obliged to do so long since.

McSwiney was clearly a dissatisfied customer, and within a year he was recorded in his native Dublin, though this is not the last we hear of him or of the Duke of Richmond in connection with Canaletto.

McSwiney's mention of Mr Smith is particularly important. It seems likely that he is referring to the same man when in the previous quote he acknowledges the help of a particular friend who, one assumes, had some influence over Canaletto. Joseph Smith was a generation older than Canaletto but died two years after him and was the most significant individual in the artist's long career. Smith was described by Horace Walpole as the 'merchant of Venice', because he had moved to the great Republic in its twilight years in order to pursue a career as a trader under the apprenticeship of Thomas Williams. He was known to almost every English visitor to Venice, it seems, and in 1744 he achieved his long-held ambition and became the English Consul in Venice. He married twice, his first wife being Katherine Tofts, who sadly suffered from occasional bouts of insanity. Almost immediately after her death he married the daughter of John Murray, who was, as Lady Mary Wortley Montagu described her, 'a beauteous virgin of forty, who after having refused all peers in England, because the nicety of her conscience

Piazza San Marco: looking West from the North End of the Piazzetta, *c. 1727.*
Pen and ink on paper, 23.4 × 18 cm
Windsor Castle, Royal Library

would not permit her to give her hand when her heart was untouched, she remained without a husband till the charm of that fine gentleman, Mr Smith, who is only eighty-two, determined her to change her condition'. This somewhat catty comment was one of many made of a man who seems to have attracted little else but derision from his fellow countrymen. On another occasion Lady Montagu asked her daughter: 'I beg you would direct the next box [of books] to me, without passing through the hands of Smith; he makes so much merit of giving himself the trouble of asking for it, that I am quite weary of him; besides that he imposes on me in everything.'

Probably cold and possibly obsequious in his kindness, Joseph Smith undoubtedly showed loyalty to Canaletto, and his brilliance as a collector should not be tarnished. However, Horace Walpole accused Smith of exploiting Canaletto and of ignorance as a collector: 'Mr Smith engaged him [Canaletto] to work for him for many years at a very low price & sold his works to the English at much higher rates', adding later that for all Smith's adulation of books, he only read the title page, and that his sophistication was skin deep. The second comment is clearly not true. Smith was known to have an inspiring library and an interest in a bookshop at the Campo San Bartolomeo in Venice. His palazzo on the Grand Canal was furnished with fine furniture imported from England and it housed his collection of pictures which was noted for its fifty Canaletto canvases, 143 Canaletto drawings, and other works by Sebastiano and Marco Ricci, Zuccarelli as well as the renowned *Music Lesson* by Vermeer. Additionally, there were wonderful coins, gems and prints. So significant was the collection that it was bought in its entirety by George III in 1762.

Though the actual correspondence between Canaletto and Smith is slim, it is evident from the pictures Smith owned that these two quiet, unobtrusive men had a long association. Of the many pictures by Canaletto that Smith owned and which are now in the Royal Collection, six views of the Piazza San Marco and the waterfront are the most stunning. Each one is vast, two being in a horizontal format and four in a vertical format, a configuration which suggests they were intended for a specific room in Smith's house. The inspired brevity with which they are painted, the warm bright sun which shines out of them and the fresh sharp sky make them perhaps the most compelling images that Canaletto ever produced (pages 61, 73, 65 and 67). The view towards San Giorgio Maggiore (page 67), most of which is given over to a wonderful sky, is made more striking by the quality of light, which is orchestrated by a series of strong diagonals running into the picture. An example is the line running from the columns of the Doge's Palace on the left towards the church of San Giorgio Maggiore in the distance, or the diagonal from the top of the St Mark's column to the top of the campanile of San Giorgio and along the line of the trees on the island. Ultimately, this picture is not a portrait of the Doge's Palace, which is barely shown, nor the church of San Giorgio Maggiore. Instead, this is a painting about light and composition and as such breaks with our normal conception of Canaletto's work.

Such imaginative views and the method of painting suggests an early date for these pictures. This is supported by the observation that the straight-sided steeple on the campanile of San Giorgio in the background was demolished between 1726 and 1728 to be replaced by an onion-shaped dome. Some years later, the dome was replaced by the present straight steeple. Canaletto frequently described the views he painted with precise topographical detail, though he was not averse to moving major features such as buildings in order to achieve a more satisfactory composition. Those who know Venice will realize that San Giorgio is, in fact, much further away than Canaletto has depicted it and also that the column of St Mark is considerably higher.

Walpole had described rather ill-temperedly what he felt were Smith's dishonest dealings with Canaletto.

However, a letter Smith sent to Samuel Hill dated 17 July 1730 shows that he, like everyone else, found it difficult to secure Canaletto's attention:

At last I've got Canal under articles to finish 2 pieces within a twelvemonth: he's so much follow'd and all are so ready to pay him his own price for his work (and which he values as much as anybody) that he would be thought in this to have obliged me, nor is it the first time that I have been glad to submitt to a painter's impertinence to serve myself and friends, for besides that resentment is lost upon them, a rupture with such as are excellent in their profession resolves 'em either not to work for you at all, or which is worse, one gets from them only slight and labour'd productions, and so our taste and generosity is censured.

It would not have been in Canaletto's interests to tether himself to an agent like Smith or McSwiney, simply because they could do no more to help him in a market which he had already cornered, being almost the only view painter in Venice and evidently the best. As the above extract suggests, Canaletto had a good idea of his own value. Even so, a loose business relationship between the two men did prove profitable. For Grand Tourists, most of whom quite probably did not speak Italian let alone the Venetian dialect, finding a view painter would have been difficult. Smith could offer considerable services. As a trader he was quite used to shipping goods and seeing them through customs. As a business man he could also finance the commission, thus relieving the patron of the worry that they might be duped and, as is clear from Smith's letter to Samuel Hill above, Smith took some care to see that standards were maintained, even at the expense of his own patience, and that the final picture was truly by Canaletto. This does not mean that visitors could not commission pictures on their own initiative, and in some cases get a better picture than Smith could acquire, but for a cautious buyer Smith was the best bet.

Walpole's charge that Smith was fleecing the English is well answered by an extraordinary and detailed account which survives regarding a pair of Canaletto pictures commissioned through Smith by the ancestors of the Earl of Wicklow:

August 22 1730 Recd two pictures of Canaletti from Venice

	£	s	d
Pd Mr Smith Mercht 35 Venn. Zecni	*18*	*7*	*11*
Freight	*0*	*11*	*0*
Custom	*2*	*0*	*0*
Charges		*8*	*0*
Frames	*1*	*14*	*0*
	23	*0*	*11*

If we assume that the charges relate to Smith's fee, then he is levying a very modest one or two per cent. It is also interesting to note from these figures that at 35 zecchini for a pair of pictures, Canaletto had not changed his prices much since 1725, even though his reputation had grown greatly by 1730.

The decade 1730–40 was the most productive period of Canaletto's career. At thirty-three years of age he was an experienced topographical painter and his only effective rival, Carlevaris, had died in 1730. Though it is difficult sometimes to trace pictures back to the original patron over two-and-a-half centuries ago, there are some notable bulk commissions which give an idea of the scale of Canaletto's turnover. For example, Lord John Russell, later the fourth Duke of Bedford, stayed in Venice while on his Grand Tour at some time between 1729 and 1731. He met Joseph Smith and subsequently acquired twenty-four views of Venice which were housed at Bedford House until 1771, when they were moved to Woburn Abbey where they can still be seen today (page 85). Although there is no surviving correspondence between Smith and the young Lord, there seems little doubt that Smith acted as agent. Lord Russell would not have been able to leave Venice with all twenty-four pictures completed and under such circumstances it would have been normal to leave the remaining business in the hands of an experienced agent in the city.

Lord Russell's brother-in-law and sister, the Earl and Countess of Essex, also visited Venice and bought six Canalettos, though unfortunately they were sold in 1777 and cannot be traced. Another group of twenty-one pictures, later owned by Sir Robert Grenville Harvey, was possibly bought by his ancestor George Grenville. The Duke of Leeds appears to have bought eleven pictures and there were seventeen Canalettos at Castle Howard until 1940, which are thought to have come from this period. In addition, Joseph Smith collected fourteen pictures and commissioned some fifty highly-finished drawings. These figures by no means represent all the pictures Canaletto painted in the 1730s, but the ninety-three paintings mentioned above give some impression of the gruelling workload undertaken by him.

There is no evidence that Canaletto employed assistants, but the poor quality of some pictures suggests that he may have accepted help, especially when one considers the intense pressure of his commitments and the detailed nature of his work. His technique of painting also changed over this period in such a way that he could work more quickly. He used a ruler more often in both his drawings and paintings and it is sometimes possible to see the pin-prick of a compass in the canvas where he marked out a dome or a circular window. The underpaint for his canvases became less sophisticated. From the views commissioned by Conti we learn that in his early work he used underpaint of differing colours for the sky or the water or buildings in a painting. From 1728, however, Canaletto prepared a uniform pale grey or beige underpaint for his canvases. In the 1720s he painted with thick impasto, giving his pictures an almost three-dimensional quality. Sometimes in the thick oily layer of paint he incised architectural details so that the scored line revealed the darker underpaint which was sufficient to delineate details that were too awkward and fiddly to achieve in paint alone. His paintings from the 1730s tend to be brighter, partly because of the light underpaint, with blue skies and generally a less vital appearance. Though wonderful for their clean, sharp images of Venice, the pictures from these years were painted for the tourist market and lack something of the moody power and spontaneity of his previous larger canvases.

Two masterpieces, *The Stonemason's Yard* (page 71) and *The Doge visiting the Church and the Scuola di San Rocco* (page 93), escape the air of drudgery of Canaletto's more commercial works. The latter painting provides a fascinating insight into the colour of a state procession as well as a glimpse of the Venetian art market, while *The Stonemason's Yard* exhibits many qualities of Canaletto's work before 1730. Painted in thick impasto, the scene is one of the most ordinary ever painted by Canaletto. Apart from the church of Santa Maria della Carità in the background, there are no important buildings depicted here and if anything the eye is drawn to the argument between members of a family on the left-hand side. This tarnished view of Venice is entirely consistent with other early work, particularly the Liechtenstein commission. Equally, one is reminded of the Conti commission and the overbearing skies which we also see in those pictures. Although nothing is known about the early history of *The Stonemason's Yard*, on the basis of style and technique alone it is thought to come from the last years of the 1720s. By 1808 it was in the collection of Sir George Beaumont, the well-known collector and champion of the arts, who eventually left it to the National Gallery, London, of which he was a founder trustee.

The assertion by Canaletto, which is related by Marchesini, that he painted in the open air becomes ever more unlikely given the number of pictures for which he was responsible. An impression of Canaletto's working method can be gleaned by an examination of his drawings. There are some five hundred drawings in total, 143 of which were in the collection of Joseph Smith. Another large collection of 138 drawings was given to the Accademia Gallery in Venice in 1949 and these form what are known as the Cagnola sketch-books.

Within the Royal Collection there is a drawing (see page 18) which is a preparatory sketch for one of the six immense paintings (page 63) of the San Marco area painted for Joseph Smith in 1727 and described earlier. This is a view of the Piazza San Marco, looking west from the eastern end by the entrance to the Doge's Palace. The drawing comes from the nascent stages of the picture. Drawn in pen and ink with strong broad strokes, it gives the impression that the artist executed it quickly with the intention of mapping out only the principal features of the painting, showing where light should fall but without paying any attention to detail in the architecture. So urgent and rapid was Canaletto's drawing that in some areas he has scored the paper, causing it to soak up excess ink like blotting paper, leaving large dark stains on the drawing.

As with the other drawings and paintings in the Smith series, the composition of this drawing relies heavily on orthogonal lines running deep into space. For example, the line created by joining the top of the two flagpoles, if extended, would cross through the furthest corner of the Piazza San Marco. Equally, the angle created by the upper edge of the balcony of San Marco on the right side of the picture, if continued, meets with the point where the Loggietta runs out of the picture on the left-hand side. This form of composition is typical of Smith's six pictures and can be observed elsewhere in Canaletto's oeuvre.

A comparison of the drawing and the finished painting makes it clear that Canaletto has altered much. Most notably, he has excluded the campanile which is quite evident in the drawing from the finished painting because it is too tall to be included given the viewpoint of the composition. It is true that Canaletto was not averse to manipulating the physical world to suit his compositions, but to have squeezed the entire campanile into this view would have exceeded the boundaries of credibility. The viewpoint for the finished picture is further to the right, creating a more acute view of San Marco and the Piazza beyond.

A similar preparatory drawing has already been illustrated in conjunction with the Stefano Conti commission, in which we detect the same speed of draftsmanship together with an additional written note as an *aide-mémoire* (see page 13). This type of sketch is a far cry from those drawings made by Canaletto in Rome between 1719 and 1720, and though it will be argued that later these were the source for paintings of the early 1740s, they do not appear to have been done as preparatory sketches. Illustrated earlier in the text (see page 10), the Rome drawings are imbued with an interest in ruins and arcadia, with foliage growing from cracks in the buildings and incidental figures adding life and charm to the composition.

Quite different from the drawings discussed above are the artist's faultless and precise sketches that are more closely linked with his working method. The drawing of the enormous Dominican church in Venice, Santi Giovanni e Paolo, relates directly to the painting illustrated on page 91. As with previous drawings, there are notes which refer to the colour to be used. For example, *coto* meaning baked, as in baked brick, is written in on the upper section of the west-facing wall of the south transept. There is also a staggered and at first confusing line running across the transept and through the building immediately to the south of the transept. If we look at the finished painting, it is immediately clear that this line is a quick notation referring to a shadow cast by the main body of the building against the setting sun.

The clear lines of this drawing and the complete absence of any fumbles have often encouraged others to suggest that Canaletto used a camera obscura (see page 24) in order to make this and other sketches. Though this is a tired argument among Canaletto

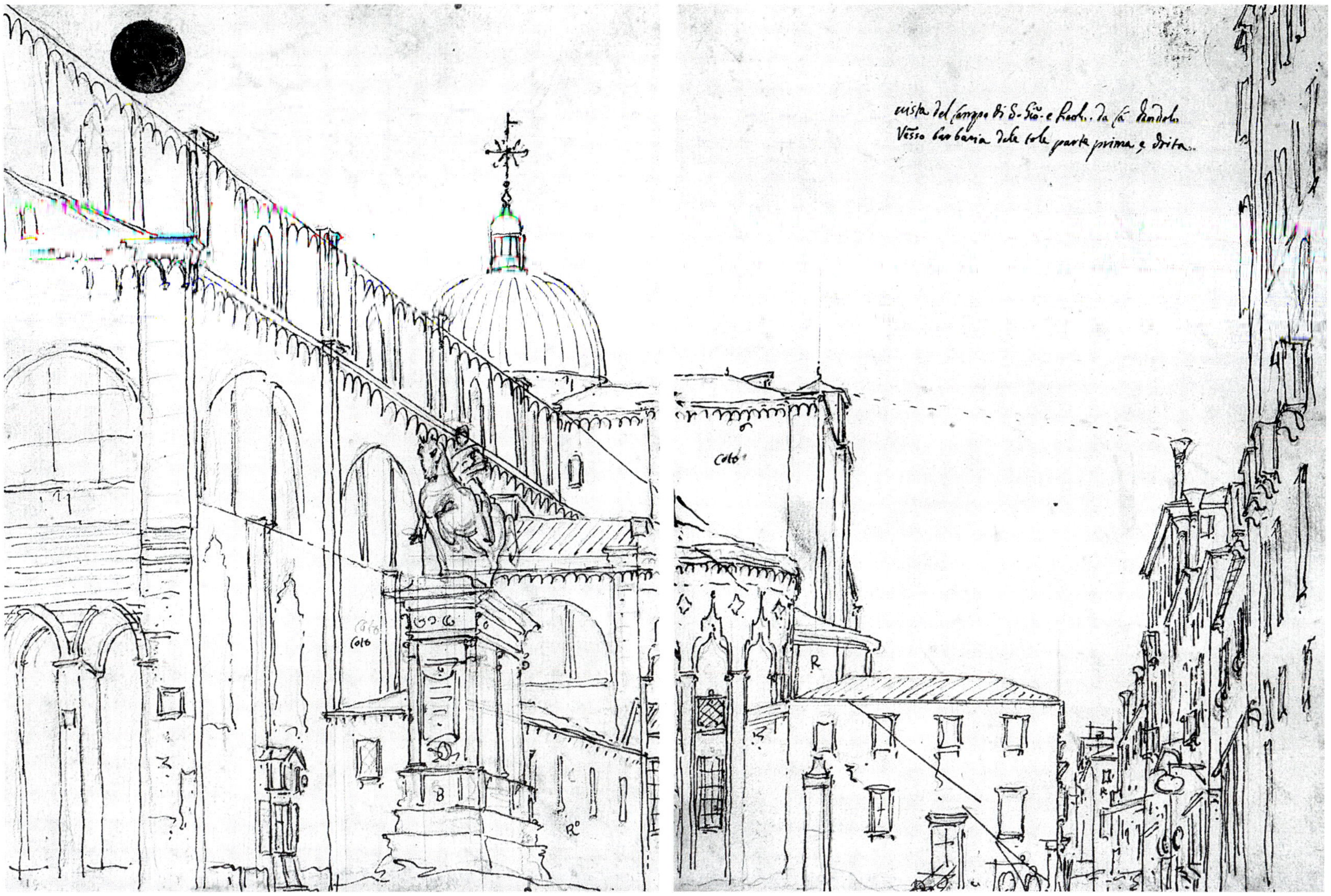

Santi Giovanni e Paolo. Two leaves from Canaletto's sketch book, *c. 1735.*
Pen and ink on paper, each 22.8 × 17 cm
Accademia, Venice

specialists, his possible use of such a camera is fascinating for anyone who marvels at the precision and detail of his painting. A camera obscura is a device used by artists to achieve an accurate image of what lies before them. Light passes through a lens at the front of a box and is reflected off a mirror set at a 45° angle within the box, casting an image across the opaque sheet of glass on the top of the box from the underside. A viewer shrouded in darkness sees, and indeed could trace, a clear if somewhat flat image. Many artists used these boxes to help them with preliminary sketches.

Had Canaletto used a camera obscura, it might be reasonable to expect some contemporary comment as he would have cut quite a curious figure shrouded under his cloak over a large box in the streets of Venice. Antonio Maria Zanetti, an early biographer of Canaletto, made an ambiguous comment on the subject, saying that the camera came with mixed blessings:

By his example Canal taught the correct way of using the Camera Ottica [obscura]; and how to understand the errors that occur in the picture when the artist follows too closely the lines of the perspective, and even more the

Photograph of the camera obscura bearing Canaletto's name
Museo Correr, Venice

aerial perspective, as it appears in the camera itself and does not know how to modify them where scientific accuracy offends against common sense. Those learned in art will understand what I mean.

One is tempted to suggest that the ink lines of the preparatory sketch for Santi Giovanni e Paolo are so clear and lacking in hesitation that Canaletto used a camera obscura. On closer examination, however, the ink lines are seen to be underdrawn with sketchy pencil lines, suggesting that a freehand drawing was made first. Additionally, other drawings of this type are not nearly so clear and accurate as those illustrated here. A camera obscura in the Museo Correr in Venice carries Canaletto's name, though there is no reason to believe that it was in fact owned by him. Ultimately there is no evidence to support the argument that he used a camera and it is the greatest testament to Canaletto's skill and ability that this argument persists.

After mapping out the sky, then the buildings and water, Canaletto would finally paint in figures who were dressed in every type of apparel reflecting the cosmopolitan nature of Venice. At no point do any of Canaletto's characters create a narrative within the picture that would distract the viewer from the beauty of the setting or the harmony that pervades his interpretation of Venice. However, by judiciously placing figures in the composition, some of them wearing bright colours, Canaletto carefully orchestrated the way in which the viewer's eye moves around the scene. A pen-and-ink drawing of such a figure exists and it would probably have been kept in a studio sketchbook for reference purposes.

While Canaletto was finding short cuts in order to keep pace with demand for his pictures, he also took steps to improve the marketing of his work by publishing in 1735 a volume of engravings after his paintings. It was called *Prospectus Magni Canalis Venetiarum* and it consisted of twelve views of the Grand Canal and two pictures of Venetian ceremonies. The title page of the book portrays Canaletto on the left and Antonio Visentini, the engraver of the plates, on the right (see page 7). This is one of the few portraits of Canaletto showing him as a young man, sporting a wig and described as 'Origine Civis Venetus' (Venetian citizen by origin), which the reader may remember is the social stratum just below the nobility. His pose and coat give him a haughty and self-possessed demeanour which presents a stark contrast with that of Visentini the craftsman.

Publications of this kind had been made before by Luca Carlevaris, for example, who published *Le Fabriche e Vedute di Venezia* in 1703 as a ploy to encourage the taste for views, and Owen McSwiney is thought to have engraved the twenty-four pictures of the imaginary tombs of English heroes to make the success of his enterprise more public. The *Prospectus* of Canaletto was a promotional exercise, and according to a letter dated 17 July 1730 from Joseph Smith to his friend Samuel Hill, the idea for such a book was formed in the late 1720s, when Canaletto had acquired a good reputation. Smith wrote to Hill: 'The prints of the views and pictures of Venice will soon be finished. I've told you there is only a limited number to be drawn off, so if you want any for friends, speak in time.'

Smith's involvement in the project was considerable; indeed all fourteen original pictures were owned by him and housed at his home, the Palazzo Mangilli-Valmarana on the Grand Canal close to the Rialto Bridge. Moreover, the publisher Giovanni Battista Pasquali was an associate of Smith in a printing firm near the church of San Bartolomeo. The first edition must have been a success, because in 1742 a second, much-extended edition in three parts was issued by the same publisher (see page 26). There were twenty-four additional engravings of the Grand Canal, various squares or campi around the city and views of the area around San Marco. These, too, were hung on the walls of Joseph Smith's home and eventually all were sold to visiting tourists except the view of Santi Giovanni e Paolo, which Smith kept back for himself (page 91).

It is difficult to be sure how many pictures Canaletto was painting each year, but on the basis of the above-mentioned ninety-three paintings, which were from bulk commissions alone, one can imagine that towards the end of the 1730s Canaletto must have been exhausted and his attitude to his work and his clients slightly jaded. It may not come as a surprise therefore that in 1740 or 1741 Canaletto stopped painting Venice. This change may have been further prompted by the War of the Austrian Succession, which made continental travel dangerous and disturbed the flow of rich tourists to Venice. Whatever the reasons, we can be sure that Canaletto went on a type of drawing sabbatical with his nephew Bernardo Bellotto during 1740–1, journeying up the Brenta Canal towards Padua. There are no diaries and no letters from either artist, so their movements have to

Study of a Standing Gentleman
Pen and pencil on paper, 29.8 × 14.4 cm
Metropolitan Museum of Art, New York

Title page of the second edition of *Prospectus Magni Canalis Venetiarum* *engraved by Antonio Visentini, 1742*

be deduced from drawings, one or two of which are conveniently dated.

Bernardo Bellotto learnt well from his uncle and later became as popular in Saxony and Poland as Canaletto was with the English. It seems reasonable to assume that Bellotto joined Canaletto's studio around 1735 when he was fourteen and that he was coming towards the end of his apprenticeship when he left in late 1741 or early 1742 to travel to Rome as Canaletto himself had done twenty years before. The young Bellotto passed through Lucca, Florence and Rome, making many drawings and painting large canvases. He came back to Venice by 1743 and is recorded as having exhibited at the Scuola di San Rocco picture market. He finally left Venice for good in 1747 to become court painter to the Elector of Saxony, where he justly acquired much fame, before eventually settling in Poland. It is a measure of his success that his pictures were sometimes confused with those of Canaletto.

Canaletto drew the lagoon north of Venice and incidental scenes en route to Padua. Most of the drawings are in pen and ink and they are often filled in with wash. One drawing (frontispiece) shows a view that looks north towards the church of San Michele in Isola on the funerary island. The lagoon has a low skyline and the water there is calm, it being protected from the open sea of the Adriatic by a series of long islands to the south which in effect create a sea wall. Within this relatively featureless landscape Canaletto has displayed his mastery of aerial perspective in order to convey a sense of depth and scale.

Although Consul Smith bought many of these drawings, Canaletto kept some back for himself, occasionally using parts of them for later pictures, as is the case with this drawing, which was used in a later painting. Attribution of these drawings is difficult because they were often accurately copied and there is, for example, another version of this view at the Ashmolean Museum, Oxford.

From the lagoon, Canaletto started up the Brenta Canal from the small port of Fusina, which lies south-west of Venice. The Canal offered a trouble-free and efficient route to Padua and beyond it into the Veneto or the Venetian hinterland. At various times since the fourteenth century the Venetians had controlled land as far as Bergamo close to Milan, which they used as a military buffer-zone throughout the intermittent wars which afflicted northern Italy during the fifteenth century. In the sixteenth century the Venetians developed this land for agricultural purposes following the decline of their sea power in the eastern Mediterranean, from where they had previously imported grain. Along the banks of the Brenta Canal, nobles and agricultural entrepreneurs built beautiful villas, many of which were designed by Palladio. In Canaletto's time, the nobility still withdrew from Venice to their country estates in the summer to bask in the cool clean air.

There is a a record of Canaletto's journey in the form of a pen-and-wash drawing of a farm on the outskirts of Padua (see page 28). This seemingly spontaneous scene, with travellers in conversation as a small coach pitches into Padua, is nonetheless contrived. The three

The Courtyard of the Castle of Konigstein from the South
by Bernardo Bellotto, c. 1756–78.
Oil on canvas, 133.4 × 238 cm
Manchester City Art Galleries

campanile in the background, which make the identification of Padua possible, have been rearranged, and it has been noted that the farmhouse is very similar to a villa near Vicenza. On closer inspection it is possible to see that the arches of the farmhouse have been scored in with a compass, while the highly-finished appearance of the drawing and its framing border suggest that this was a studio drawing.

Over the same period Canaletto made another exciting departure from his established métier by publishing a set of etchings, on which the dedication by Canaletto to Consul Smith was personalized 'as a mark of esteem and homage' (see page 29). The etchings range over Canaletto's sojourn, illustrating small towns on the Brenta, imagined views and some prospects of Venice. It is a mark of Canaletto's skill that he could adopt a new medium with easy grace and produce etchings of such arresting strength. One etching shows a contrived view of a backwater of the lagoon, with Venice across the water in the background. The sentiment of this etching is most like *The Stonemason's Yard* in that there is no dominating edifice and the scene is principally given over to daily occupations and the activities of a boatyard in the middle distance. Significantly this etching is dated 1741, which means that Canaletto temporarily left Venice, even though the volume dedicated to Smith was published in 1744. Also from the same series of etchings is the view titled *Pra' della Valle*, a huge open space in Padua (see page 29).

In 1742 Canaletto signed and dated five enormous paintings depicting scenes from Rome, two of which are shown on pages 99 and 101. They were commissioned by Joseph Smith and, on the basis of their size,

Farm on the Outskirts of Padua, *c. 1740–41*
Pen and wash on paper, 31.4 × 39.9 cm
Windsor Castle, Royal Library

they were probably intended for Smith's palazzo on the Grand Canal or for his country house in the Veneto. The subject matter of these pictures raises speculation that Canaletto went to Rome at this time, though this is difficult to endorse because neither Canaletto's biographers nor customs documents give any hint that he made such a journey. Despite this mystery, it is possible to piece together sources for these views. When Canaletto had visited Rome with his father during 1719–20, he had made a number of finished drawings, including one of the Arch of Septimius Severus (see page 10). This scene and two others of the five paintings, are represented in the surviving drawings from his earlier visit to Rome. The two remaining sources could have come from Bernardo Bellotto who, as discussed above, had travelled to Rome in 1741–2 and had brought back with him a number of drawings and canvases which Canaletto may have used for his own work.

One of the most interesting facets of Canaletto's œuvre is a group of paintings called *capricci*. Words like 'caprice' and 'capricious' have the same root, meaning unaccountable or whimsical changes of mind. In this sense, a capriccio by Canaletto is a curious and fanciful assembly of buildings such as never existed in reality. Having trained as a set designer with his father and worked on Owen McSwiney's imaginary tombs, such inventions must have been almost second nature to Canaletto, although his invented scenes of the 1740s are much the most entertaining and amusing.

Yet again Joseph Smith was involved. He commissioned thirteen capricci to be 'Pieces over doors [to] contain the following most admired Buildings at Venice, Elegantly Horizoned with Figures and Adjacencys to the Painters Fancy', which were probably intended to be set within his palazzo on the Grand Canal or his country house at Mogliano. The quality of these pictures varies considerably, but two of the best are illustrated on (pages 103 and 105).

A capriccio, as Canaletto paints it, is a visual and intellectual game relying heavily upon the erudition of the spectator. A good example (see page 30) shows the Rialto Bridge in Venice as Andrea Palladio, the great sixteenth-century architect from Vicenza, had once designed it (although he did not get the commission to build it), nestling between two buildings in Vicenza also designed by Palladio. This painting was probably commissioned by Francesco Algarotti, who

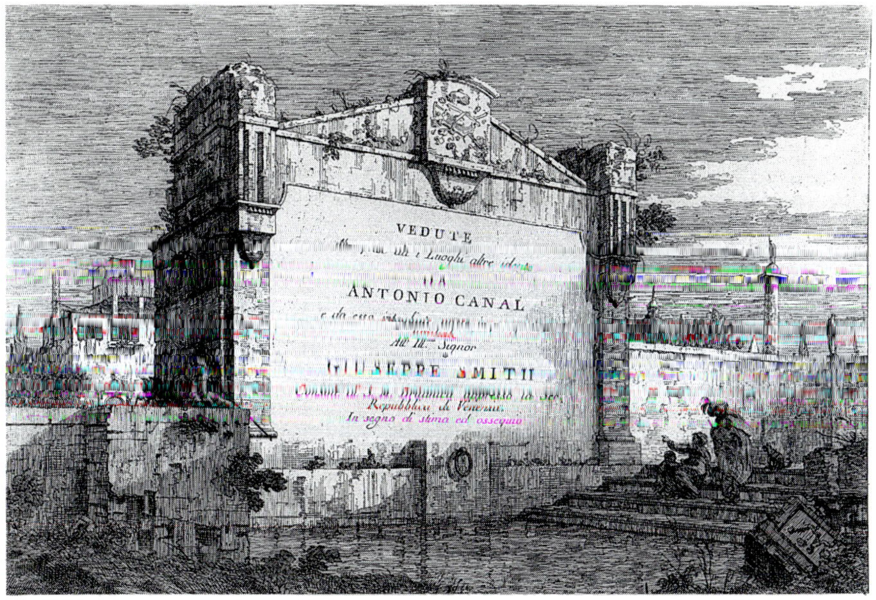

Three etchings from a series produced for Joseph Smith published in 1744: title page showing a dedication to Joseph Smith; a view of a town with a harbour; Pra della Valle.
Courtauld Institute, London

wrote in 1759 about a picture that sounds very similar: 'To the right, in place of the Fondaco, we put the Palazzo Chiericati by the same Palladio . . . and in the middle there stands the Basilica of Vicenza, known as the Palazzo della Ragione.'

The years 1740–4 are perhaps the most interesting in Canaletto's career because of the great technical versatility he displayed and the vast range of subject matter he explored. It is very clear, however, that he relied almost entirely upon the patronage of Joseph Smith, a situation which could not last. In 1744 Canaletto was forty-seven, and it must have become clear that he needed to change course if not venue.

Capriccio, Grand Canal: a Palladian Design for the Rialto Bridge with Buildings at Vicenza, *c. 1742–44*
Oil on canvas, 60.5 × 82 cm
Private Collection

In 1746 Canaletto left Venice for England. During the years leading up to his departure, his life was troubled by an unseemly and scarring family squabble in the courts, the death of his father in 1744 and a decline in the tourist trade which affected the market for topographical pictures. Indeed, after 1741 his only consistent patron was Joseph Smith, who in 1744 became the British Consul to Venice and could thus be assumed to have less time for erudite pursuits such as Canaletto's painting. As if to confirm the low ebb of Canaletto's career, he had been ignored by Francesco Algarotti, who was the buying agent for the Elector of Saxony and had recently visited Venice.

Many Venetian artists had moved abroad before him; Giovanni Battista Tiepolo, Giovanni Antonio Pellegrini, and his own nephew, Bernardo Bellotto, had all done well. Jacopo Amigoni, a Neapolitan painter who had settled in Venice, gave Canaletto much encouragement, having returned from ten profitable years in England. Canaletto also had many advantages. All but a few of his pictures had been bought by Englishmen and, with the help of Consul Smith, Canaletto could look forward to a reputation that preceded him and to the boon of friends at court.

The first we hear of Canaletto's move to London is from George Vertue, a diarist of the mid-eighteenth century and a constant source of reliable gossip:

*Latter end of May came to London from Venice the Famous Painter of Views Cannalletti [*sic*] . . . of Venice. The Multitude of his works done abroad for English noblemen & Gentlemen has produced him a great reputation & his great merrit & excellence in that way, he is much esteemed and no doubt but what Views and works He doth here, will give the same satisfaction – though many persons already have so many of his paintings.*

For Canaletto to find a market in England was, nonetheless, a daunting prospect. As Vertue points out, many people had bought from Canaletto before and if Smith and McSwiney are to be believed, English patrons had often been badly treated by the artist, suffering long delays and variable prices. Canaletto might have consoled himself with the thought that most of his erstwhile patrons owned several houses and thus might wish to cover acres of wall space. The artist was, however, unlikely to know what Smith and McSwiney had written about him, especially if they had exaggerated his truculent behaviour in order to placate impatient clients or even to polish their own reputations as diligent and resourceful servants of nobility. George Vertue gives an alternative reason for Canaletto's move to England:

It's said he has already made himself easy in his fortune and likewise that he had brought most part to putt into the Stocks here for better security or better interest than abroad.

It may have been true that stocks in England were more stable and profitable than in Italy, but security would have been more difficult to maintain, and Canaletto might have encouraged upbeat rumours in order to screen his urgent need for patrons.

During May of 1746 Canaletto arrived in London, where he found a population of approximately 900,000, a low flat skyline punctuated by many church spires and towers, and the broad River Thames. William Hogarth provides us with a potent image of mid-eighteenth-century life in England in which we see an acute contrast between rich and poor. This was accompanied by an aggressive air of entrepreneurship sweeping the fortunes of many along on a roller-coaster of self-interest and gain. The heady atmosphere of the South Sea Bubble and the massive fortunes amassed by daring commodity trading worldwide helped to build the fibre and the resources for the later nineteenth-century empire. Unlike the rigidity of the Venetian class system, society in England was volatile and peopled with individuals eager to appropriate the trappings of refined society and good taste. As a foreigner coming from an older and more sophisticated society, Canaletto could expect some kudos for his work which would, when bought, imply the erudition of the subsequent owner.

There were great houses in London, many of which he was later to paint, but London did not possess great administrative buildings of the grandeur to which he had become accustomed in Venice. There was no dominating governmental precinct like the Doge's Palace and the Piazza San Marco, no treasury like Sansovino's mint, and few open spaces traversed by exotic traders and flamboyant bureaucrats. As a Venetian it seems natural that Canaletto should have gravitated towards the River Thames, which coincidentally had become a focus of attention because of the controversy surrounding the building of a new bridge across the water.

London had long needed a further bridge across the Thames. Since 1111 the City of London Bridge had served the east end of the city, and in 1729 a wooden structure was built at Fulham, but for several decades plans had been advanced for a new route to be thrown across at Westminster. Some demolition was required, particularly on the north bank, but the commercial and long-term benefits of such an enterprise were clear. The south side of the river was underdeveloped, with only a ribbon of building along the bank past the occasional, important site like Lambeth Palace. A barrage of criticism assailed the plan launched by the Fathers of the City of London, who were anxious that the focus of the city should not go to the west. The waterboatmen, 30,000 of them, would clearly be out of a job, as well as many publicans, who presumably profited from the well-being of the waterboatmen. This unlikely alliance of interested parties formed a powerful lobby which obstructed progress and made the issue of the bridge a very live one. Eventually the foundation stone for the bridge was laid in 1739, and by the time Canaletto arrived in 1746 the project was thought to be nearing completion. Unfortunately, settlement meant that one of the arches had to be dismantled in 1749.

A drawing shows a view of the north bank of the Thames looking west. At the centre of the picture is Westminster Abbey with St Stephen's Hall, which is

London: the Thames Looking Towards Westminster from York Stairs, *c. 1749*
Pen and wash on paper, 29 × 45.5 cm
Yale Center for British Art, New Haven
Paul Mellon Collection

today incorporated within the New Palace of Westminster. The large wooden structure on the right is a water-tower for the supply of water to the large houses along that part of the Embankment. Immediately to the right is the landing jetty for the Royal Dower House, Old Somerset House. On the far left of the drawing is the bulky castellated form of Lambeth Palace and to its right, and most significantly, the new Westminster Bridge.

Though it is generally accepted as a drawing by Canaletto, there are some immediate problems with the view shown because Canaletto has not drawn the bridge as it looked in the summer of 1746. By 1744 the bridge was almost finished and the north bank had already been reached well before Canaletto's arrival. The Swiss engineer Charles Lebelye took the unusual course of starting the bridge at the middle bay and then building towards the banks, eight arches each way. Some say that in the drawing Canaletto has shown the bridge touching down on the north side, in which case he has omitted three arches. The author does not think that the bridge has reached the north bank but he cannot imagine how Canaletto expected to draw three more arches in the remaining space.

It is possible that Canaletto was using someone else's drawing or engraving as a source, but no such image has come to light. We have, however, become accustomed to Canaletto manipulating topography in order to serve the composition of a picture and he has perhaps done the same here. If Canaletto had drawn the bridge as it was in 1746, the left side of the picture would quite possibly be rather weak and without punctuation. This hints at a larger problem that Canaletto may have faced in that the Thames is considerably wider than the Grand Canal and such a low, broad skyline made for uneventful pictures.

Canaletto's first patron, according to the diaries of Horace Walpole, was Baron Lobkowitz, a Bohemian nobleman who had come to England in the summer in 1746 to buy livestock for his stables. Two views of the Thames are now housed at Dresden and even though the history of these pictures cannot be traced further back than 1752, it seems quite possible that the baron bought them in 1746. These two pictures do confirm Canaletto's interest in the Thames shortly after his arrival in England, even though it is slightly ironic that his first patron in London should be Bohemian.

Canaletto had used engravings in Venice as a way of publicizing his work, and it is interesting to note that within months of his arrival he was doing the same in England. In 1747 the publisher John Brindley released two engravings: one shows the Lord Mayor's Day festivities near Westminster Bridge and the other is a view of the Thames looking east towards St Paul's, which is seen through one of the arches of Westminster Bridge (the paintings are reproduced on pages 113 and 111). The use of the arch of the bridge as a frame is an extraordinarily imaginative compositional device and an ingenous way of solving the difficulty that Canaletto faced with the low skyline of London and the need to bracket the scene in some way.

The owner of this picture of the Thames was Sir Hugh Smithson, who soon became one of the most significant patrons of Canaletto's sojourn in England. He was a Yorkshire squire when, in 1741, he married Lady Elizabeth Seymour. Four years later, her brother died and suddenly Smithson and his new wife were catapulted into the highest and oldest ranks of nobility. By her brother's death, Elizabeth Seymour attracted six baronies and four Percy seats (Northumberland House, Syon Park, Petworth and Alnwick Castle). Later through his father-in-law, Sir Hugh Smithson acceded to the earldom of Northumberland later taking the title of Duke of Northumberland, thus becoming a very influential man.

Canaletto had arrived in London with one letter of introduction from Joseph Smith, which he duly delivered. Smith had been very astute in realizing that perhaps erstwhile patrons of Canaletto would be unlikely to want more paintings and that, on the basis of information from agents like Smith himself, many patrons had a jaundiced view of the Venetian painter. He therefore omitted to write to any of his more obvious contacts. Instead, Smith wrote to Owen McSwiney, whom he knew not only as a flamboyant entrepreneur but also as an agent for the second Duke of Richmond. Richmond was one of the few patrons who had Canalettos which were not topographical views of Venice. McSwiney subsequently mentioned Canaletto to Thomas Hill, the Duke's old tutor, who in turn wrote to the Duke:

The only news i know to send you, is what i had this day from McSwiney at the Duke of Montagu's where we dined, & he, I think got almost drunk. Canales, alias Canaletti, is come over with a letter of recommendation from our old acquaintance the consul of venice to Mac in order to [have] his introduction to your Grace, as a patron of the politer arts or what the Italians understand by the name of virtu. I told him that the best service I thought you could do him w'd be to let him draw a view of the river from yr dining-room, which in my opinion would give him as much reputation as any of his Venetian prospects.

Hill's letter was sent on 20 May 1746, yet it is a year before we hear of Canaletto drawing the views from Richmond House. The two finished canvases, *London, the Thames and City of London from Richmond House* (page 115) and *London: Whitehall and the Privy Garden from Richmond House* are perhaps the greatest pictures he painted while in England.

Throughout 1747, 1748 and 1749, Canaletto had some good commissions, though it is not clear in what order these pictures came. From an entry in Vertue's diary of 1749 we learn that Canaletto had done work for the Duke of Beaufort at Badminton, painting the prospect from the garden front, while on 19 July 1748, Hoare's Bank records show that Canaletto was paid £58 by Lord Brooke, later the Earl of Warwick, for perhaps two of five paintings which survive of Warwick Castle. Then, on 3 March 1749, Canaletto received £31 10s for one of two views of the east front in the same collection. During the same year Canaletto was commissioned by Joseph Wilcocks, the Dean of Westminster, to paint the procession of the Knights of the Order of Bath which took place on 2 June (page 117). A month later, on 2 July, Sir Hugh Smithson, who had by then inherited the Percy seats mentioned above, wrote to his mother-in-law that Canaletto was painting Syon House, a short distance to the west of London, and that 'by the outlines upon the Canvass I think it will have a noble effect and he seems himself to be much pleas'd with the subject which i should think will suit his manner of painting perfectly well.'

In spite of the success Canaletto was having in locating a rich seam of patronage, George Vertue makes a disturbing note in his diaries in June 1749:

On the whole of him something is obscure or strange, he does not produce works so well done as those of Venice or other parts of Italy. which are in the Collection here. and are done by him there. especially his figures in his works done here, are apparently much inferior to those done abroad. which are surprisingly well done & with great freedom & variety-his water and his skies at no time excellent or with natural freedom. & what he has done here his prospects of Trees woods or handling or pencilling of that part not various nor skilful as might be expected. above all he is remarkable for his reservedness and shyness in being seen at work, at any Time, or anywhere. which has much strengthened a conjecture that he is not the veritable Canaletto of Venice. whose works there have been bought at great prices. or that privately, he has some unknown assistant in making or filling up his pieces of works with figures.

The view put forward by Vertue must have been in common currency, because a month later Canaletto took the unusual step of placing an advertisement in a London newspaper, the evidence for which we again derive from Vertue: 'Signor Canaleto [sic] hereby invites any gentleman that will be pleased to come to his House, to see a picture done by him, being A View

London: Northumberland House *c. 1752*
Pen and wash on paper, 29 × 42.5 cm
Minneapolis Institute of Arts

of St James's Park, which he hope may in some Measure deserve their Approbation . . . at his lodgings Mr Wiggan Cabinet maker in Silver street Golden Square' (now 41 Beak Street, which runs east off Regent Street today). By this method Canaletto must have hoped to scotch those damaging rumours. As far as Vertue was concerned, it clearly worked:

at last after some time I heard how that difficulty, was spread about . . . it seems his name and family was canali – so he was called – he had a sister who had a son who having some genius. was instructed by his uncle Cannali. and this young stripling by degrees came on forward in his profession being taken notice of his improvements he was Cannaleti – the young. but in time getting some degree of merit. he being puffed up disobliged his uncle who turned him adrift. but well Imitating his uncles manner of painting became reputed and the name of Canaletti was indifferently used by both uncle and nephew at Venice so that this caused the report of two Canalettos which was this manner.

A clue to the original source of these rumours may be found amongst the papers of Edward Dayes. Even though he was born in 1762 and he was writing at second or third hand, he may relate something of the truth in this matter:

The picture dealing tribe carried their assurance so far, as to deny that Canaletti was the person who painted his pictures at venice, that is, on his arrival at London and when, by the provocation, he was tempted to sit down and produce some to convince the public, they still persisted that the pieces now produced were not in the same style; an assertion that materially injured him for a time and made him almost frantic. By this scheme they hoped to drive him from the country, and thereby to prevent him detecting the copies they had made from his works, which were in great repute.

Whether bothered by rumours and bad publicity or for some other reason, Canaletto returned to Venice late in the summer of 1750. We can only guess at the intended permanence of his trip by what Canaletto did in Venice. On 8 March 1751 he bought the lease of a building on the Zattere called the Scuola dei Luganegheri for 2,150 ducats or £360. Such a sum in England would buy six Canalettos at £60–£70 a picture, according to Vertue in 1751. For Canaletto, six pictures was a good year's work and it therefore seems odd that after five years in England he did not have much to invest. However, by taking out the lease on the Zattere he had a sure rent from the sitting tenants, the Scuola dei Luganegheri, of 602 ducats per annum, producing an impressive return of a little under 30 per cent, which perhaps formed the foundation of his pension.

While in Venice, Canaletto renewed his association with Joseph Smith and, in 1751, a third edition of *Prospectus* was published, probably in an attempt to arouse interest in the ageing artist. If this was the intention, the ploy clearly failed, because by the summer of 1751 we hear from Vertue of Canaletto's return to England. On his arrival Canaletto took out another advertisement in a London evening newspaper inviting the public to his studio to view a picture of Chelsea College, Ranelagh Gardens and the Rotunda. Unfortunately it brought some savage criticism from Vertue, who commented; 'it is tho't that this View is not so well as some of Canaletto formerly brought into England. nor does it appear to be better than some painters in England can do'. This picture, however, did arouse the interest of engravers, in particular Nathaniel Parr, who engraved views of festivities at Ranelagh, while Robert Sayer and Henry Overton published four views of Vauxhall Gardens in December 1751. Both Ranelagh and Vauxhall Gardens were pleasure parks and the manner in which Canaletto was choosing subject matter that might be of interest to anyone who suggests that he was finding it ever more difficult to secure private patronage.

Despite these difficult times, Canaletto was able to rekindle the interest of some previous patrons. In March and July of 1752 there are notes of payments made out to Canaletto from Hoare's Bank on behalf of Lord Brooke for the two remaining views of Warwick Castle. Lord Brooke remained a particularly loyal patron of Canaletto, as did the Duke of Northumberland, formerly Sir Hugh Smithson. By 1752 Northumberland House had undergone some renovation and its new occupant commissioned Canaletto to paint a portrait of it, the drawing for which is illustrated (see page 35).

The drawing of Northumberland House is particularly fascinating, because this vast edifice was torn down in 1873 to make way for Northumberland Avenue. The house was built on a large quadrangle on top of the old palace of Whitehall and it is hard to imagine that it had a positively huge garden running down to the Thames. To the left of the drawing are a number of shops and other businesses which have been identified as The Mews Coffee House, Widow Bagnall's Saddler's Shop and the Cannon's Street Eating House. Northumberland House is set at a slightly different angle in this drawing when compared with the finished picture, but there cannot be much doubt that they are preparatory study and finished work.

There is a suspicion that Canaletto made his way back to Venice around 1753 for another short visit before returning to London once more. A normally reliable contemporary diarist, Pietro Gradenigo, mentions Canaletto's visit even though there are no customs records or details of what he did there in that time.

It is quite clear, however, that Canaletto was in England in 1754, because he inscribed the back of six pictures for Thomas Hollis with this signature and 'done in London in 1754 . . .'. Hollis was an interesting man, quite out of keeping with Canaletto's normal lordly patrons, and his choice of subject matter was equally idiosyncratic. A radical with republican sympathies, a supporter of the fledgling America and a significant benefactor of Harvard University, Hollis was also a friend of Joseph Smith in Venice. He met him between December 1750 and February of the following year and maintained a correspondence with him until Smith died, leaving Hollis some books in his will. Hollis, who was a collector of books, prints and engravings was, no doubt encouraged by Smith, to collect Canalettos too.

Unlike other patrons, Hollis had no theme to his collection of Canalettos – no clutch of estates to portray, no notable prospects to illuminate. Instead, Canaletto painted the Piazza del Campidoglio from another artist's engraving. Then, from a picture of the interior of the Rotunda at Ranelagh Gardens painted three years previously, Canaletto reproduced the scene for Hollis (page 127). There is a view of St Paul's, a capriccio of Whitehall and a view of the north side of Westminster Bridge under repair, *c.*1750. Most importantly, though, Canaletto painted

Piazza San Marco: looking East from the South-west Corner
Pen and brown ink on paper, 228 × 333 cm
Metropolitan Museum of Art, New York

Old Walton Bridge (page 125) for Hollis, and in this work Canaletto arguably gets closest to painting an English landscape with English eyes.

There is a further collection of six paintings which is thought to come from this late period and is known as the Lovelace collection, so called because the pictures were sold in 1937 by the Earl of Lovelace, a descendant of the third Lord King, who is said to have commissioned them. Each one is a capriccio, four of them being smaller pictures of quasi-Italian/Venetian scenes and two of them larger landscapes in which

Capriccio with Roman Triumphal Arch and Ruins
Ink, wash and pencil, 38.4 × 54.4 cm
Metropolitan Museum, New York

Italianate buildings are set into an apparently English landscape (page 133). As such they seem to make a set which may have been intended for the decoration of a room and are similar to the large views of Rome painted by Canaletto for Smith in 1742.

In all, Canaletto spent eight years in England, with

one or perhaps two breaks to visit Venice. He painted between forty and fifty paintings. Although he began by painting views of the Thames, more than half of his work was devoted to estate portraiture, views of public entertainment and ceremonies. As a Venetian aged forty-nine, arriving in London presumably without speaking much English, it was a remarkable achievement that he was able to find enough patrons to enable him to paint five or six canvases each year.

Canaletto returned to Venice in 1755 with few prospects. Interest in him had evidently run dry in England and the likelihood of finding English patrons in Venice would have been remote for the same reasons. Aged fifty-eight, he still needed to work, having only a small income from the lease on the building occupied by the Scuola dei Luganegheri. To make up the shortfall, he did repeats of successful and well-known paintings, such as *The Bacino di San Marco on Ascension Day* (see page 89). He also used old drawings for small portable pictures for the tourist market. For example, there is a drawing (see page 37) of the Piazza San Marco looking to the east of which he used the right side for a small painting now in the National Gallery, London. It is clear, however, that the drawing was made before 1753, and thus before he went to England, because the clock-tower on the left-hand side does not show alterations which were completed in that year. As another source of income, Canaletto drew highly polished capricci, one of which juxtaposes a triumphal arch at Pola, which Canaletto had never seen but knew from an engraving by Piranesi, with the tower of a Gothic church somewhat reminiscent of those in England.

Although there is little information about Canaletto's later life, there is one intriguing anecdote published in 1856, long after his death, which sheds some light on his lifestyle. The Reverend Edward Hinchcliffe recorded that in 1760 his grandfather was walking with John Crewe in Venice when:

[He] chanced to see a little man making a sketch of the Campanile in St Mark's Place; Hinchcliffe took the liberty, not an offensive one abroad, as I myself can testify – to look at what he was doing. Straightaway he discovered a master-hand and hazarded the artist's name 'Canaletti'. The man looked up and replied 'mi conosce' [you know me]. Thereupon a conversation insued, and Canaletti, pleased to find so enthusiastic a judge of drawing, invited Hinchcliffe to his studio, who waited upon him there the following day, and inspected his paintings and drawings. The visit terminated most agreeably to the traveller. Having requested Canaletti to allow him to purchase the

Piazza San Marco: looking East from the South-west Corner, *1760*
Oil on canvas, 69 × 60.5 cm
Private Collection

painting about to be made from the sketch he had seen the artist take, Canaletti not only agreed to this, but, in addition, presented him with the sketch itself, as a complimentary gift.

A view of the Piazza San Marco looking east (see page 39) was sold in 1836 by a member of the Crewe family, and it seems that one part of Hinchcliffe's story is true. The sketch, however, has never been located, although there is a rather polished drawing of the same view, which is still with the family. Whether or not entirely factual, the story is useful since it is feasible that Canaletto had taken to drawing in the street, particularly around the Piazza San Marco, in order to attract the attention of passing tourists. It is certainly true, for example, that John Crewe did buy a large canvas of London: *Whitehall and the Privy Garden looking North* from Canaletto in 1760, possibly on the visit mentioned above. The picture was subsequently bought in 1839 by the Duke of Buccleuch and still hangs today at Bowhill.

Canaletto could no longer rely on the patronage of Joseph Smith, who in 1760 had retired from his post as Consul and by all accounts had developed a rather jaundiced view of Venice and had even considered a return to England. James, the brother of the famous Scottish architect Robert Adam, had visited Smith during the same year and had commented that the latter was 'devilish poor and should he live a few years longer, which he may do, will die a bankrupt'. Smith was evidently also in financial straits and had begun negotations to sell his huge collection of five hundred pictures, fifty of them by Canaletto, to George III, a deal which he completed in 1762 for £20,000. Smith died in 1770, but even though he had money in his last years he rarely lavished it on Canaletto, commissioning only one painting of the interior of San Marco and a few drawings.

One of the greatest ironies of eighteenth-century Venetian painting is that perhaps its best-known son was turned down by the Accademia di Belle Arti (Academy of Fine Arts). Founded in 1756, the Accademia was a teaching institution, a regulatory body and a purveyor of establishment taste. It had thirty-six permanent members, who elected new artists when and if space became available. Canaletto was not involved with its foundation and in 1763 he was passed over when three places became available. He was beaten to his place by two forgotten painters, Pietro Gradizzi and Francesco Pavona, while Francesco Zuccarelli was rightly elected. The two now unknown artists were probably preferred to Canaletto because they were both figure painters and thus further up the creative scale. In September of the same year, another position became available and Canaletto was elected, but with four votes against out of an electing committee of fourteen. Two years later Canaletto presented an elaborate capriccio (page 139) as his official reception piece. His offering goes beyond topographical painting towards a more intellectual approach to composition, incorporating spatial dynamics within the picture. This might have been an attempt on Canaletto's part to raise the standing of cityscape painting from that of the simple copyist to that of a creative artist.

Canaletto's last recorded act was that he attended a meeting at the Accademia in 1767. He died in 1768 suffering from an inflamed bladder and was buried in his home parish of San Lio on 19 April. The 'brilliant and celebrated master', as the Accademia's citation had read, left almost nothing: twenty-eight unsold paintings, a single bed, two bed covers and, as the executor of his will described them, 'some old cloths'.

As an artist, Canaletto still baffles onlookers with the detail within his pictures and the warmth of the sunlight which shines within them. He was succeeded in Venice by Francesco Guardi, but in Eastern Europe his nephew Bernardo Bellotto continued this tradition of fastidiously detailed painting. In England he influenced Samuel Scott and William Marlow during his own lifetime, and after his death Bonington, Turner, Samuel Prout and James Holland.

Venice: Piazzetta di San Marco
by Francesco Guardi, after 1780.
Oil on canvas, 72.4 × 118.7 cm
National Gallery, London

The only direct comment from this inscrutable man which reflects in any way on him personally concerns a drawing from 1766 which depicts the choir singing in San Marco. Canaletto has signed the drawing underneath, noting that he was sixty-eight years old and that he had done it 'without glasses'. On the basis of one comment it is impossible to fathom the artist's character and sadly for him most secondary sources unite in finding him disagreeable. However, the author believes that the magnitude of his detractors' dislike of him was directly proportional to the intensity of their desire to own one of his paintings. Having begun with an eighteenth-century eulogy, it seems appropriate to finish with another, from Antonio Zanetti the Younger, one of Canaletto's biographers:

In his pictures Canaletto combined nature and artistic licence with such skill that his works appear absolutely accurate to those who judge them only according to the principles of good sense; but those with real understanding will find in them great judgement in the choice of views, in the distribution of figures and space and in the arrangement of light and shade – as well as beautiful clarity and vitality and ease of colour and brushwork; the effects of a serene personality and happy genius.

1697 ❧ 1768

A. Canal f.

THE PLATES

This is arguably Canaletto's first view of Venice. The date of it can be assumed because some newly laid paving can be seen in the middle of the piazza which corresponds with a design by Andrea Tirali planned in 1723 that replaced the ridged, drained brick surface seen elsewhere in this painting.

In style, Canaletto's brushwork is brief and smudges over the fine detail of the architecture in order to give an overall atmosphere of this immense square. There is a sense of bustling activity in the market in front of San Marco which, together with the goat herd in the far left-hand corner of the piazza, seems inappropriate to the dignity of the surrounding buildings. Worse still are the torn and dishevelled awnings on the Procuratie Vecchie which lurch and pitch as if drunk. Canaletto has painted an honest view of a place he knew well and his picture provides a dramatic contrast to his later prospects of Venice.

Straight ahead is the Basilica di San Marco which, since 1807, has been the cathedral of Venice, although it was originally founded in 832 to be the doge's private chapel. Built over several centuries, it is a jumble of Byzantine, Romanesque and Gothic architecture, the richness of which is a reminder of the long and prosperous history of the Venetian Republic. It is covered with trophies of military conquest and trading power. Above the west door it is possible to see the tilting heads of the four bronze horses which were brought to Venice from the Hippodrome in Constantinople after the 1204 Crusade.

Although Canaletto was mistakenly admired for his dextrous depiction of the world as we see it, he should never be underestimated for his ability to tailor reality to suit his own compositions. In this picture he changed the angle of the two flanking buildings in order to create a more dynamic view. Likewise he shrank the campanile to fit it into the canvas, but his most audacious folly was to leave out one of the five domes of San Marco.

Piazza San Marco: looking East

Painted 1723

142 × 205 cm

Thyssen-Bornemisza Collection, Lugano

The Rio dei Mendicanti is the canal that runs down the side of the Scuola di San Marco. In the middle of this picture, to the left of the bridges, one can just see the back of the Scuola's high arched façade. Though the Scuola was much visited, this Rio would be an unlikely walkway for the Grand Tourist. Indeed the large white façade of the principal building to the left is arguably a poor focus for a picture. It was the Mendicanti, the orphanage described by William Beckford when he spoke of the quality of the female choirs in Venice and it is possible, therefore, that this picture was commissioned by a Venetian who had some involvement with the institution, rather than by a visitor. In support of this argument, the size of this canvas is far greater than any other exported by Canaletto. Even though this picture and its companions found their way to the Liechtenstein collection, it is conceivable that they were commissioned by an early patron of Canaletto, probably a Venetian.

In common with other paintings from the 1720s, this picture is scattered with figures involved in daily pursuits such as the boatyard workers on the right, the cloth-dyers under the bridge, the old man resting against the Mendicanti on the left and the younger man relieving himself against the church façade.

Rio dei Mendicanti: looking South

Painted c.*1723*

143 × 200 cm

Ca' Rezzonico, Venice

An Allegorical Painting of the Tomb of Lord Somers

Painted c.1722–29
279.4 × 205 cm
Viscount Windsor

Commissioned by Owen McSwiney between 1722 and 1729, this is one of twenty-four pictures depicting fanciful architectonic tombs of great heroes of England, two of which involved Canaletto. McSwiney had no specific patrons in mind at the outset of this scheme but he did sell ten pictures to the Duke of Richmond, who played a significant role in Canaletto's career.

This picture is not characteristic of Canaletto's known work, though the strong element of fantasy is in some respects a return to his early training as a set designer. He was one of three artists involved, painting only the architecture, while the landscape was done by G.B. Cimaroli and the figures by G.B. Piazzetta. Each picture in the series was executed by at least three artists, which must have created a logistical nightmare that is strangely fitting for this extraordinary concept from the eccentric McSwiney.

The tomb is for Lord Somers, 1651–1716, who was Lord Chancellor of England, best remembered for his steadfast adherence to the reformed faith and his defence of seven bishops who were brought to trial for sedition by James II. The adulatory theme for this scheme glorified English heroes who were particularly involved with the Protestant faith and the establishment of the new order that followed the Glorious Revolution of 1688. It is curious to note that the Duke of Richmond bought part of a series which celebrated the demise of his own blood relation, James II.

The tomb is to the right-hand side and is surmounted by allegorical figures representing justice and peace, while in the bottom centre of the picture we see an unidentified but presumably grateful bishop before the tomb of his advocate.

The Grand Canal: Rialto Bridge from the North

Painted 1725

91.5 × 134.5 cm

Private Collection

This picture is one of a set of four commissioned by Stefano Conti, which forms one of the most significant groups of pictures from Canaletto's early career. As discussed in the text, both the correspondence between Alessandro Marchesini and a preparatory drawing survive, giving us an invaluable insight into the working method of Canaletto.

In order to be sure of his merchandise, Stefano Conti demanded a description of the scene from the artist himself:

. . . the bridge of the Rialto on the side looking towards the German Warehouse which is opposite the palace of the Magistrates of Camerlinghi [sic] and other Magistrates besides, looking down upon the Vegetable Market where they land all kinds of the Vegetables and fruits to be shared amongst the dealers in the City. In the middle of the canal is painted a Perotta Nobile [a nobleman's barge] with figures in it and four gondolas going at full speed and close to a Gondolier having the Livery of the Emperor's Ambassador.

With seeming innocence, Canaletto drew Conti's attention to a nobleman's barge with its scarlet awning and the gondola of the Emperor's ambassador. The same ambassador had just bought a painting by Canaletto from the San Rocco market and the inclusion of his gondola seems to be a reference to the prestigious nature of Canaletto's patrons.

The Rialto area was the fulcrum of Venetian trade and therefore of the city's power. It was not only a general-purpose food market, but also centre of the city's financial institutions. For example, the Palazzo dei Cameralenghi was occupied by the city treasurers. To the left side of the picture, the beige palace bathed in sunlight is the Fondaco dei Tedeschi, which acted as a warehouse and trading centre for German commodity brokers.

The Grand Canal: looking North from near the Rialto Bridge

Painted 1725
90 × 132 cm
Private Collection

This is the pendant to the picture of the Rialto Bridge from the north, painted in 1725 for Stefano Conti. The view here seems to be taken from the same window, but more to the right in order to show the Fabbriche Vecchie or vegetable markets. Beyond, in a splash of morning sunlight, it is possible to see the open-air fishmarket and the throng of traders. On 3 August 1780 William Beckford described this scene thus:

It was not 5 o'clock before I was roused, by a loud din of voices and splashing water, under my balcony. Looking out, I beheld the Grand Canal so entirely covered with fruits and vegetables, on rafts and in barges, that I could scarcely distinguish a wave. Loads of grapes, peaches and melons arrived, and disappeared in an instant; for every vessel was in motion, and the crowds of purchasers hurrying from boat to boat formed one of the liveliest pictures imaginable.

Compared with its pendant, this picture is unavoidably less interesting as it does not have the dramatic advantages of the sweep of the Canal or the Rialto Bridge. What Canaletto lacks in scenery, however, he makes up for in a most dramatic cloud, with a single hanging cumulus, making it one of his best skies. Bruised skies and green moody water are elements of his early work, together with incidental details of ongoing life. In this picture, such a detail is the scaffolding attached to the Fabbriche Vecchie towards the left-hand edge of the painting.

Although there are no workmen present in this scene, they do appear in its pendant, tottering as they tile the roof. To link two pictures in such a modest and unassuming way is charm itself and must have convinced Stefano Conti that he had made the right choice in commissioning Canaletto instead of Carlevaris to paint the views.

Santa Maria della Carità is the church featured in *The Stonemason's Yard* (page 71), but in this picture we are looking at the façade. To the right is the last stretch of the Grand Canal, which comes to an end by the church of Santa Maria della Salute, whose dome can also be seen in this picture. One bridge in the foreground no longer exists, because the canal which flowed under it was filled in, along with many others, by Napoleon's government after the fall of the Republic in 1797.

This large canvas is one of those commissioned by Stefano Conti through Alessandro Marchesini. It was the last to be finished in the series and the final account was settled on 15 June 1726. As promised at the outset of the commission, Canaletto provided a description:

The church of the Patri della Carità Rochetini with its campo where I have disposed many small figures amongst which, in a little group of three figures in the centre of the campo, are two priests of the same order who are discoursing with a learned man in a violet-coloured robe. On the horizon at the farther end of the canal is part of the Riva degli Schiavoni. The cupola which is seen is the principal one of the church of the Salute, the lower part of which continues as far as the Dogana di Mare (marine customs house).

Canaletto, however, reproduced the subject matter of this scene several times, thus ignoring Conti's demands that this should be an exclusive painting.

The Grand Canal: from Santa Maria della Carità to the Bacino di San Marco

Painted 1726
90 × 132 cm
Private Collection

Santi Giovanni e Paolo and the Scuola di San Marco

Painted 1725
125 × 165 cm
Gemäldegalerie, Dresden

This picture was probably bought in 1725 by the ambassador of the Holy Roman Emperor from the market outside the Scuola di San Rocco. We know this from Marchesini's correspondence with Stefano Conti and it seems likely that on hearing of the calibre of Canaletto's patrons, Conti increased his order from two paintings to four. Subsequently this view became well known because it was frequently copied.

The scene is of the Scuola di San Marco straight ahead and the church of Santi Giovanni e Paolo to the right. The Scuola was one of the five major confraternities distributed around Venice; it was an association of men who, though not drawn from one trade or necessarily from one class, were dedicated to good works and the collective care of the members. So, for example, a recently widowed mother might expect help from her deceased husband's scuola. Each member paid an annual fee which over a period of time made some scuole particularly rich. For the ordinary citizen, the scuole provided a system of assurance and an opportunity to lobby the Consiglio Maggiore through the heads of the scuole, who were generally from the nobility. The scuole therefore became an important organ of the state and it is largely due to their existence that Venice suffered few severe bouts of insurrection, which is surprising when we consider that only one or two per cent of the population governed the whole. The Scuola di San Marco was the most prestigious and the richest scuola, with a magnificent building in the most affluent quarter of Venice. Near to San Marco and the Rialto, this area would have been one of the most frequently visited by the tourists.

San Giacomo di Rialto

Painted c.*1725–30*
95.5 × 117 cm
Gemäldegalerie, Dresden

Although the patron of this picture is not known, it was one of five that were eventually owned by the Elector of Saxony. This view is of a different size from that of the other four in the Saxony collection, suggesting that it was bought on its own. It depicts the square (or campo) just behind the Rialto Bridge over the Grand Canal. The evening is drawing in and, judging by the angle of the shadows, the time must be shortly before dusk, although Canaletto has raised the sun artificially high because at that time the entire campo would be swamped in shadow. Deep within those shadows is the Ruga degli Orefici, or gold and silver market, while in the campo itself there is a rich mixture of Moors, Turks, Venetians and tourists. A noble, caped in black and wearing a wig, barters with some picture-sellers in front of San Giacomo, while another has just bought a bird from some poultry-sellers, in the foreground. The central aisle of the bridge with its shops is carefully observed by Canaletto, with tradesmen's signs hanging over the heads of the passers-by.

The sunlit square is still today used as a market, though not as a forum for picture salesmen and poultry-sellers as shown by Canaletto. The interesting variety of animated figures and incidental vignettes of daily life such as washing on the façade of San Giacomo are typical features of Canaletto's painting up to 1730. On the basis of style alone, for that is the only information we have, this is probably an early picture by the artist, given the variety of figures and the slightly 'off-beat' subject.

This area was the first to be settled by the Venetians, partly because it is in the centre of the islands that make up Venice, and secondly because it is an area with a high bank, or Ri(vo) Alto. The church of San Giacomo, though much restored, is one of the oldest in Venice and its position at one end of the market reminds one of the arrangement of buildings at Covent Garden in London.

This is one of six large paintings for Joseph Smith, commissioned *c.*1727. It is a view of the south-west corner of the Piazzetta looking at Santa Maria della Salute past Sansovino's Library. On the right-hand side is a monumental column surmounted by St Theodore, who was the patron saint of Venice before his position was usurped by the better-known and more important St Mark. At the foot of the column there is a collection of animated figures, seemingly from every part of the world. On the far right is a splendid oriental gentleman, and sitting down facing the viewer is an older man wearing a short tubular hat, reminiscent of those worn by men on the Dalmatian coast. Just to the left of this group, with his back to us, is a Venetian wearing a three-pointed hat, a powdered wig and a sky-blue cape, which signifies that he is a Sapie, or member of the judiciary.

The brief brushstrokes and vivid sky and clouds are features of Canaletto's work in the 1720s. It hardly seems as if this is a picture of the Library or Santa Maria della Salute or indeed of St Theodore, especially when one considers that two-thirds of this large picture is dedicated to sky. What is striking, however, is the triangular composition of the work, a feature which runs through the other five pictures in this series. Some of the three following views are more successful than this, but it leaves one wondering what Canaletto might have achieved had he not been swamped by the English Grand Tourist market and the commercialism which that involved.

Santa Maria della Salute is a church that celebrates in flamboyant style the end of the 1640 plague. Designed by Baldassare Longhena, it is a constant reminder of the building achievements of the Venetians, principally because it is founded on more than 1,700,000 piles.

Entrance to the Grand Canal: from the Piazzetta

Painted c.1727

170 × 135.5 cm

Royal Collection

This picture is linked with a drawing in the text (see page 18) and a comparison of the two reveals some changes made by Canaletto: for example, in the finished picture he has taken a more acute angle in his view of the Piazza San Marco. Additionally, he has not included the campanile, even though there is a shadow of its presence along the left-hand edge of the picture. In terms of composition, triangular and orthogonal lines are clearly present, while the figures in the foreground are included to present a sense of scale. Similarly, there is a considerable proportion of canvas given over to the sky. As we look past the gallery of the front of San Marco, we see the immense length of the Procuratie Vecchie for the Procurators of San Marco. Procurators were civil servants and their building was a series of offices conveniently close to the main government chambers inside the Doge's Palace. One of the responsibilities of the procurators was to oversee the maintenance and particularly the appearance of the San Marco precinct.

Within any city, to have such large open space was a considerable luxury and, as if to recognize this, Napoleon described the Piazza San Marco as the greatest drawing-room in Europe. The state, however, did not squander funds, but arranged this assembly of administrative buildings during the sixteenth century in order to demonstrate to visiting ambassadors the power and civilization of Venice. The potent mixture of the Doge's Palace, the seat of government, a treasury, the judiciary, the church and the great seat of learning at the Library must have greatly impressed, if not daunted, lesser men.

Piazzetta San Marco: looking West from the North End of the Piazzetta

Painted c.*1727*

170 × 129.3 cm

Royal Collection

The Piazzetta: looking North

Painted c.1727
170.2 × 129.5 cm
Royal Collection

Those familiar with Venice will surely know that the view in this picture is quite impossible. The Basilica di San Marco, for example, has been moved like a chess knight, both forwards and sideways, towards the viewpoint in the west of the square. The Doge's Palace has been completely ignored, while the clock-tower and archway directly in front of the viewer have been moved backwards. Canaletto has thus made the square larger and smaller in different directions and has consequently created a more dynamic picture. The figures within the Piazzetta follow the same format as in other pictures from this series; the bewigged man in the foreground wearing a crimson garment is a senator.

On the left-hand side of the picture we see the corner of Sansovino's Library. This was begun in 1537 in order to house a famous collection of books from Nicea, given by Cardinal Bessarion. It took many years for the procurators of San Marco to clear a congregation of salami- and cheese-sellers who used to occupy this site. Eventually the library was constructed in a classical style of white Istrian stone, in striking contrast to every other building in the Piazza and Piazetta. This shift in architectural style perhaps represents a change of focus by Venice from the eastern Mediterranean to Italy, following the fall of Constantinople in 1453.

Moving to another part of the Piazzetta, Canaletto has painted the last three bays of the Doge's Palace, a column surmounted by a winged lion, which is the emblem of St Mark, and in the distance the island and church of San Giorgio Maggiore. In common with the other pictures in this series, Canaletto has used a strong triangular composition. There is also a wonderful honeyed evening light reflecting off the façade of the Doge's Palace. The beauty of this is in no way diminished by the liberties taken by Canaletto with the natural world in order to fashion a memorable picture. For example, if the Doge's Palace on its west side is bathed in sunlight, why then is the façade of San Giorgio Maggiore, which faces the same way, in shadow? Additionally, a shadow is cast across the left-hand bay of the Doge's Palace as we see it, but in reality there is no building which could cast such a shadow.

The Doge's Palace was the ceremonial home of the doge and the headquarters of the legislative chambers, the Consiglio Maggiore, the Council of Ten and the judiciary. The site for this building goes back to the ninth century but the building itself has been altered or rebuilt several times. Despite many Renaissance changes, the Doge's Palace retains a particularly Venetian appearance, merging Byzantium with northern Europe. Capitals carved with Romanesque simplicity and arches shaped in Gothic quatrefoils mix with the patterned brickwork of the Orient.

The Piazzetta: looking South

Painted c.1727

170.2 × 132 cm

Royal Collection

Painted in oil on copper, this picture is smaller than those already mentioned and represents a new format of cityscape promoted by both Owen McSwiney and Joseph Smith. Bought by the Earl of Leicester, this picture represents an early example of paintings sold to Grand Tourists. It was portable, and copper would survive the three-week journey back to England.

As the only bridge across the Grand Canal, the Rialto Bridge was an essential part of the city's infrastructure. Together with the administrative precinct of San Marco, the Rialto Bridge would have been much visited by Grand Tourists. Spanning the Grand Canal, it joins the market and financial institutions to the main walkways towards San Marco. It is a remarkable bridge, with a central aisle lined with shops running between two outer walkways. Shoppers can dawdle along the central aisles, while those wishing to cross the bridge quickly, or needing to service the shops, can do so by the two outer walkways. The previous bridge was a wooden construction, also with shops, and this was replaced by the work of Antonio da Ponte at a cost of 250,000 ducats, between 1588 and 1592, after the government had turned down designs from other architects, including Michelangelo, Sansovino and Palladio.

The scene is painted as if in the early evening sun and the picture is dotted with languid figures enjoying the cool of the day. The sky is blue and bright and in many respects this represents a 'tidied up' view of Venice, except for the figure relieving himself in the right-hand corner of the staircase.

The Grand Canal: Rialto Bridge from the South

Painted 1727

45.5 × 62.5 cm

Holkham Hall, Norfolk

The Grand Canal: 'The Stonemason's Yard'

Painted c.1728

124 × 163 cm

National Gallery, London

The Stonemason's Yard is one of Canaletto's most loved and yet confusing pictures. In many respects this picture is not typical of eighteenth-century painting as it depicts ordinary life with a degree of squalor which Canaletto normally reserved for drawings and sometimes engravings. To have devoted a large canvas to a scene with no evident meaning or notable architectural subject seems strange. The site will be known to those who have visited Venice. The church straight ahead is Santa Maria della Carità and to its right is the scuola which today houses the Accademia Art Gallery. There have, however, been some changes since Canaletto's view: the campanile of Santa Maria della Carità fell down in the 1740s and the small pale buildings shown in sunlight are now replaced by one end of the Accademia Bridge.

The mystery of this picture is that the original patron is unknown and therefore we have no date. The painting finally found its way to George Beaumont, an English connoisseur and collector who left it to the National Gallery, London, in 1823. On the basis of the impasto paintwork and the undefined subject matter, it is normally assumed that the picture dates from the period 1725–30. For decades it has been titled *The Stonemason's Yard*, though there are no records to suggest that such a workshop ever existed on this site, which implies that the makeshift shed and scattered Istrian marble are part of an ongoing building site. As in other early paintings by Canaletto, the figures that populate the cityscape are animated and are a constant source of fascination. Each person is involved in some argument, conversation or task, and the most endearing is a child who is out of control.

The Bacino di San Marco: looking East

Painted c.*1726–38*
124.5 × 204.5 cm
Museum of Fine Arts, Boston

Along with *The Stonemason's Yard* (page 71) and *The Doge visiting the Church and Scuola di San Rocco* (page 93), this view of the Bacino is broadly accepted as a masterpiece by Canaletto and, like the pictures mentioned above, the precise details of its commission and date remain a mystery.

Until 1939, when W.G. Constable, the first great scholar of Canaletto, directed Boston's Museum of Fine Arts towards the purchase of this picture, it was part of a collection of Canalettos at Castle Howard. Tradition has it that the fourth Earl of Carlisle collected at least seventeen pictures by the Venetian scene-painter before the former's death in 1758. Though some of his pictures were good, others were apparently far from the standards which make attribution to Canaletto acceptable. It seems unlikely, therefore, that Joseph Smith was involved as an agent because, generally speaking, those commissions in which Smith was involved are of a consistently high quality. It is also fair to say that Smith did not allow true masterpieces to slip his grip, and if the fourth Earl did buy this picture, Smith was probably not aware of its existence.

The Bacino is the natural basin which forms the vestibule of Venice. Merchants and ambassadors would approach Venice via the Lido and the Guidecca, on the far right of the picture, coming towards the Doge's Palace and the looping domes of the Basilica di San Marco. Looking around, they would see the church of San Giorgio Maggiore, which is the white façade towards the right of Canaletto's canvas, and the great dome of Santa Maria della Salute which is behind the viewpoint of this picture. Thus visitors were presented with a view of the centre of an empire which was strong in the defence of its realm but approachable, beautiful and civilized in appearance.

Canaletto has taken his view from the Punta di Dogana, the spur of land which sharpens to a point and which is marked by a golden weather vane. As in so many of his pictures he has tweaked reality to fit the picture frame while distracting our critical eye filling the foreground with almost every conceivable craft and boating activity. Three-masted lateen-rigged ships bearing the flags of Venice, Denmark, France and England list idly in the waters, while more traditional Venetian craft scurry around the lagoon. To the left, docked in front of the Doge's Palace is the dormant Bucintoro shrouded in covers, perhaps awaiting the next Ascension Day procession.

Though no documents survive for this picture, it is possible to date it to within ten years thanks to the accuracy with which Canaletto paints in details. For example, the pointed spire of San Giorgio Maggiore was replaced between 1726–8 by an onion-shaped dome as depicted here. Also, Canaletto has shown on the skyline of the Riva degli Schiavone, to the left of the picture, the campanile of San Antonin shrouded in scaffolding. The final payment for this building work was made in late 1738.

This picture of Piazza San Marco looking north towards the Torre dell'Orologio (the clock-tower) was an attempt on the part of Canaletto to achieve a much greater degree of accuracy in his portrayal of San Marco and its precinct.

Comparison with the six paintings of the same area he made for Smith shows that Canaletto has here taken a close-up view of the Loggia and clock-tower, and he has not tampered with the positioning of buildings to achieve a more dynamic or satisfactory composition. In many respects this painting represents the transitional stage between the 'off-beat' views of his early career and the more tourist-orientated subject matter dictated by commercial demands. The format of this and later paintings is evidence for his use of geometric instruments to speed up production. Canaletto's pictures became more painstaking as he changed from working in thick impasto to a much thinner paint which was better for painting fine detail. This time-consuming technique may seem paradoxical next to his evident desire to capture the tourist market, but when one considers that visitors wanted a 'photographic' reproduction of Venice rather than an artist's impression, it was a very astute move.

Piazza San Marco: looking North

Painted c.1729

53 × 70.5 cm

The Nelson-Atkins Museum of Art, Kansas City

Similar to the view of the Molo looking west, commissioned by Samuel Hill, this picture is painted on copper and has a format suitable for freight back to England. It is one of several bought by the Duke of Devonshire in the early 1730s. In many respects it shows a marked departure from Canaletto's style in the 1720s. The sun shines brightly and there are few elements of daily squalor about this attractive scene.

Canaletto has taken the view for this picture from an imagined spot about fifteen feet above the Grand Canal. The viewer looks towards the Doge's Palace and beyond to the prison, past the column of St Mark and the column of St Theodore. Between these two columns, enemies of the state were hung for the populace to see. Other forms of execution included drowning with the aid of a heavy weight, in an area of the lagoon which even today fishermen do not trawl. Indeed, behind the agreeable arcades of the Doge's Palace, a collective consciousness of determined self-preservation dispensed rough and apparent justice. It is, after all, a curious piece of town planning to have a grand prison built of expensive stone by the side of the seat of government.

Riva degli Schiavoni: looking East

Painted c.*1730*

26 × 62 cm

Devonshire Collection Trustees, Chatsworth

This view of the interior of San Marco is an unusual picture for Canaletto, for it is one of only three interiors that he painted throughout his long career. In addition, it is quite a small picture and its subsequent ownership by Joseph Smith suggests that it might have been specially commissioned.

This is a truly wonderful composition because the pier of the crossing dome anchors the picture two-thirds of the way across the painting, creating diagonal spaces both in front and to the side of the viewer. Perspective is created by the immense looping arch of the crossing and the top rail of the iconostasis or rood-screen. A comfortable warm light floods from the left of the picture, glancing off the heads of the congregation and clergy and reflecting off the cross and golden ornaments. The source of this light causes some confusion, because it can only have come from the west doors and window. As such, the sun must be setting and the service attended must be an evening one. What is strange is that no light shines down from the two fenestrated domes towards the top of the picture. Canaletto has again tampered with reality in order to create a memorable and arresting picture.

It is also impossible to identify which service is taking place, because none of the figures represented is anything more than a blob or a sticky dash of paint. It is a testament to Canaletto's technical ability that he can create so much out of so little and his use of paint in this picture makes it possible to date it to the period 1725–30. It should be noted that Canaletto has scored the paint while still wet to create detail, such as the saints' rail at the top of the iconostasis.

San Marco: an Evening Service

Painted c.*1730*

28.6 × 19.7 cm

Royal Collection

Like so many of Canaletto's paintings before 1730, this picture presents a number of problems. In terms of what we expect from Canaletto, this is a surprising view for him, and it is painted with a particularly loose style of brushwork. An evening view, this picture shows the island of Murano in the far distance and the church of San Michele, with its 'pepper pot' exedral chapel and dome. In the foreground, bathed in bright sunlight, is the church of San Cristoforo, which was demolished when the island of San Michele was made into a municipal cemetery in the nineteenth century.

There are no records that enable us to date this picture, but on the basis of style alone there are a number of hints. For example, the thick impasto painting style is reminiscent of the interior of San Marco, particularly in the area around the façade of San Cristoforo. It is also possible to see the grey and red underpaint, known to be used by Canaletto before 1728, which shows through some rough and scumbled brushwork in the sky. The choice of subject matter, however, encourages one to consider two periods of his life, either the period up to 1730, or during 1740–1, when he took a sabbatical from the Grand Tourist trade, to travel up the Brenta. It is true that there are many drawings of the lagoon from this later period and indeed there are also capricci which incorporate the same area, but the spirited brushwork is very reminiscent of his early career, a time in which he undertook many varied subjects from *The Stonemason's Yard* (page 71) to *A Puppet Show on the Piazzetta* (page 83).

San Cristoforo, San Michele and Murano: from Fondamenta Nuova

Painted c.*1725–30*

142.2 × 150.5 cm

Dallas Museum of Art

A Puppet Show on the Piazzetta

Painted c.*1725–30*
24 × 31 cm
The Ashmolean Museum, Oxford

Even those well versed in the works of Canaletto may find this picture surprising. It depicts a puppet show taking place on the Piazzetta outside the Doge's Palace. This is the only painting by Canaletto which makes any reference to street theatre or carnival celebrations other than those officially run by the state, such as the Regatta and the Ascension Day Festival. It is curious that this should be the only picture by him which remotely refers to the Venetian Carnival, an event that was almost inescapable, as it lasted from Christmas to Shrove Tuesday.

The loose paintwork and thick impasto of the paint suggest that this is a picture from his early career. In addition, the red underpaint shows through some patches of the sky, a feature of his early work which has already been discussed. The argument for an early date is supported by the sharp steeple on the campanile of San Giorgio Maggiore, which was known to have been demolished during 1726–8 and replaced by an onion-shaped dome. It is true that the onion dome was subsequently replaced by a straight-sided steeple, but that was in the late eighteenth century, after Canaletto's death. Though there is no conclusive proof that Canaletto painted this picture, a survey of his achievements in the 1720s makes it clear that he was capable of such lucid paintwork and varied subject matter.

The small size of canvas and its poor preparation suggest that he may have painted this scene for his own amusement. Furthermore, it is possible to see the weave of the canvas, which in itself would be unusual for Canaletto if this picture was for public sale, because generally his preparation of canvases was extremely careful.

This picture is one of twenty-four bought by the Duke of Bedford shortly after he visited Venice in 1731, and it can still be seen today at Woburn Abbey. It is a view of the main gate into the Arsenale, or naval boatyard of Venice. The productive power of this yard was staggering; for example, during one year in the late sixteenth century it produced one hundred fighting galleons in sixteen days. Many of the dry docks still survive and the present Italian navy has a small base there.

Venice relied on the strength of her navy in order to secure the freedom of passage for her trading fleets into the eastern Mediterranean. There was always a danger of piracy from the north African coast and, after the fall of Constantinople in 1453, there was need for even more vigilance. Piracy was detrimental to Venetian trade in two ways. Not only was the loss of life and property distressing and inconvenient, but the disruption to timetables, delivery dates and the co-ordination necessary for profitable trade was disabling. The desire for the maintenance of regularity and predictability is borne out in one way by the shippers' adherence to the ancient galley design for their trading vessels long after the successful development of the large, faster sailing ships in northern Europe. This was not mindless conservatism but pragmatism, for galleys were not subject to the whim of the wind and could run to an exact timetable.

The Arsenale: the Water Entrance

Painted c.*1732*

46 × 78.8 cm

Woburn Abbey

A Regatta on the Grand Canal

Painted c.*1733*
77 × 126 cm
Royal Collection

This remarkable picture is one of three paintings by Canaletto which depict major public festivals. It is the Regatta which can be held on either 2 February or 26 December, St Stephen's Day. It is a great public celebration for which the oarsmen, who are seen rowing up the Grand Canal, practise even today. The course for the race is from the east of Venice along the Grand Canal to its end, and back to the Volta di Canal, the turn in the Canal shown here.

The attention to architectural detail is staggering, yet there are precious few clues as to the identity of the individuals involved or the precise year of this event. To the far left of the picture there is the *macchina*, which was a temporary structure set up on the corner of the Grand Canal in the form of a triumphal arch from which the doge had the best view of the race. Under the baldacchino of this structure it is just possible to see the red and white of a coat of arms. This is assumed to be the coat of arms of Carlo Ruzzini, who was doge from June 1732 until January 1735. The fact that this picture was engraved and included in the fourteen plates for Canaletto's first edition of *Prospectus* published in 1735 makes it more probable that Ruzzini was indeed the attending doge. Several figures are seen wearing white carnival masks, which suggests the later date of 2 February 1733 or 1734. This picture was once owned by Canaletto's patron and dealer, Joseph Smith, and is now in the collection of Her Majesty the Queen.

The Bacino di San Marco on Ascension Day

Painted 1732
77 × 125 cm
Royal Collection

This picture of the Ascension Day celebrations in Venice was also published in the first edition of *Prospectus* and owned by Joseph Smith. The celebrations refer back to *c.*1000 when Doge Pietro Orseolo II launched a fleet against the Dalmatian pirates, who were disrupting Venetian trade. The campaign was a notable success and because it began on Ascension Day, it was celebrated annually as a sign of Venice's unity with the sea. To perpetuate this *sposalizio del mare*, the reigning doge set out in a massive ornamental barge into the lagoon from the Molo and throws a gold wedding ring into the sea, so marrying Venice to the sea and securing good fortune for another year.

This *Bucintoro* (ship of gold) was the last ever built and Canaletto has painted it in all its magnificent grandeur and weighty decoration. Venetian wits apparently used to muse that one day this immense, top-heavy and unstable vessel would capsize and thus consummate Venice's marriage to the sea.

There are one or two notable changes in style from Canaletto's work of the 1720s, primarily that at the time he painted this picture he used a thinner consistency of paint which enabled him to paint detail with exacting precision rather than alluding to form as he had done with thick impasto brushwork in his early career. The overall appearance of this picture is also brighter and less moody. The sky is blue, and the canal no longer has the bile-green depths that are visible, for example, in his pictures for Conti (pages 14, 51, 53, and 55). Instead, Canaletto paints choppy waves in short-hand and without depth in a way that does not bear close scrutiny. In sum, this picture and that of the Regatta are triumphs of detail and of the portrayal of activity, presenting a truly brilliant image of Venice.

Santi Giovanni e Paolo and the Monument of Bartolomeo Colleoni

Painted 1735
46 × 78 cm
Royal Collection

This painting was owned by Joseph Smith and is the only picture he held back for himself following the publication of the second edition of *Prospectus* in 1742. Two drawings in the text are preparatory drawings for this picture (see page 23).

The scene shows the great Dominican Church of Santi Giovanni e Paolo and to the left, the Scuola di San Marco. In the middle of the square is the bronze monument to Bartolomeo Colleoni, by Verrocchio. Such a monument was particularly rare in Venice because the Venetian government and people veered towards anonymity and away from the pursuit of personal fame. Colleoni was a mercenary who fought brilliantly on behalf of Venice and, on his death, he left money for the erection of a monument. Perhaps calculating the discomfort this would cause, he specified that it should stand before San Marco in the Piazza. With adroit ingenuity the authorities did as he had asked, unveiling his portrait in front of the Scuola di San Marco.

This picture has a clever composition. In the foreground, one's eye is attracted by the senator wearing a red cape. From there the eye runs back to another senator in a similar red cape, just at the door of the church. At this point the eye either runs diagonally up a strong shadow towards the top of the Scuola di San Marco or up the verticals of the façade to the top of Santi Giovanni e Paolo. Running along the roof line of the nave, the eye joins another diagonal shadow across the transept, moving back to the ground level and the narrow street disappearing into the distance. The bottom corner of this diagonal shadow also meets with a white marble step which traverses the length of the piazza, bringing the eye back to the foreground. By this method Canaletto, almost indiscernibly, transports the viewer around his painting.

Canaletto's picture of the doge's visit to the Scuola di San Rocco is unlike much of his work, because people play almost as great a role in the picture as the architecture. It is one of three pictures which describe a public ceremony or festival in Venice. The doge made an annual visit to the Scuola di San Rocco on 16 August, which is the feast day of San Rocco. This ceremony attracted many, including Venetian nobility and visiting ambassadors. It may be because this ceremony occurred during the holiday period following the major festival of the Feast of the Assumption, on 15 August, that the tradition of an art market in the piazza outside the church and Scuola was started. Art markets were not a particularly common occurrence, since, as a rule, artists painted pictures under commission rather than in the hope of a sale. It was from this market that the ambassador to the Holy Roman Emperor bought a view of Santi Giovanni e Paolo, which we know of from a letter to Conti.

The Scuola di San Rocco is, like the Scuola di San Marco, one of the five principal scuole of Venice. In legend, San Rocco was miraculously cured of leprosy, but in Venice he was closely associated with plague and as such he was very important, since the city had a flawed fresh water supply and consequently was frequently afflicted by plague. As with so many scenes by Canaletto, the specific identity of figures depicted is tantalizingly obscure. Indeed, the patron for this picture is also a mystery, making a precise identification and date more elusive.

The Doge visiting the Church and the Scuola di San Rocco

Painted c.*1735*

147 × 199 cm

National Gallery, London

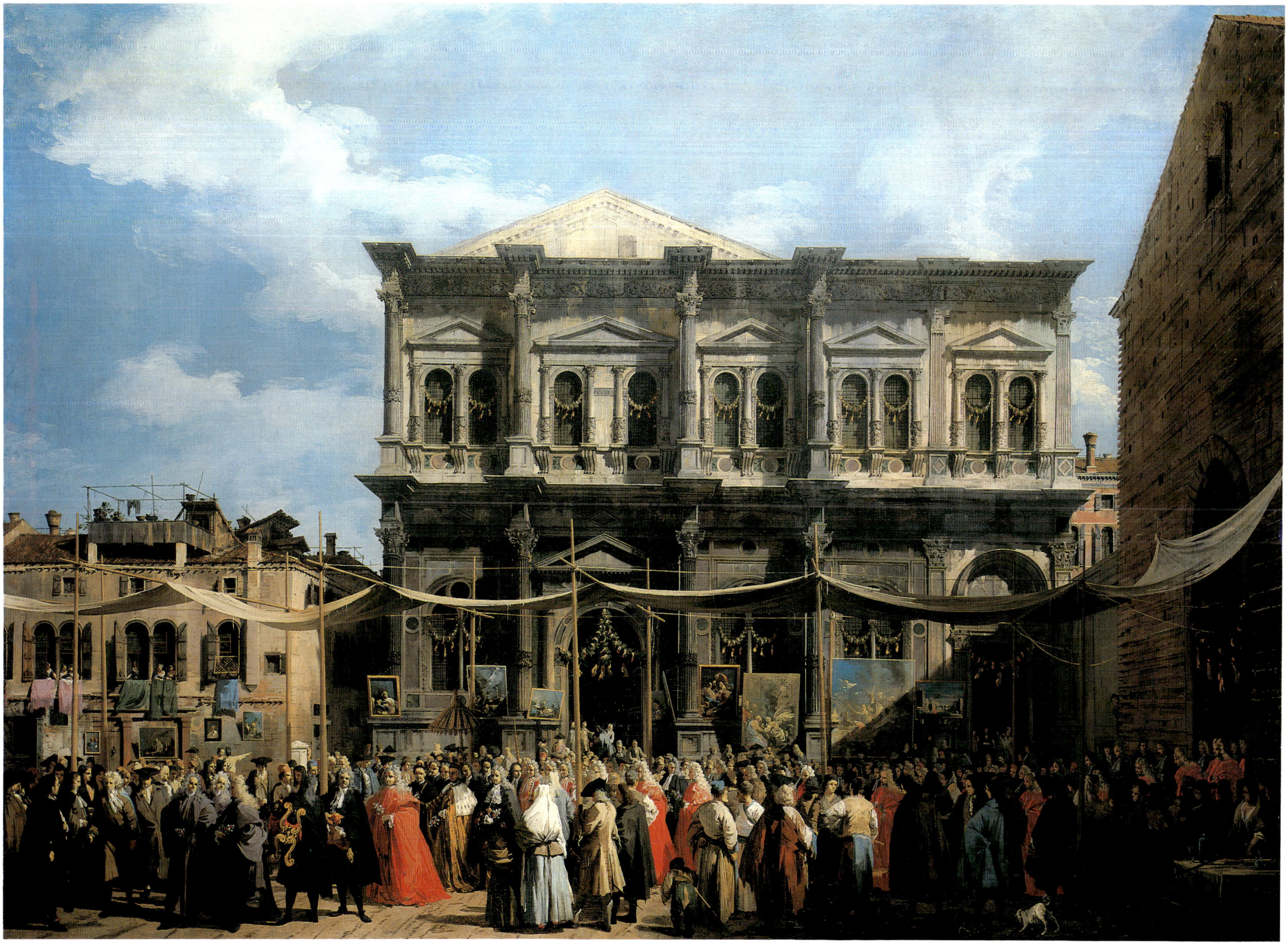

Similar to the painting of the Piazza San Marco looking north (page 75), this is a picture for the tourist market, being of a smaller size with carefully and accurately depicted architecture. It was bought between 1735 and 1740 by the Earl of Carlisle together with sixteen other pictures by Canaletto. The quality of Carlisle's pictures is far from consistent, but his dislike of Joseph Smith drove him to seek another, though less reliable, agent.

This unusual view of San Marco illustrates well the main ceremonial buildings of the Venetian state. State processions were a frequent occurrence in Venetian life, with each parish, and many other churches, receiving a visit each year. Such processions were generally an observance of a feast day, but they also served as a demonstration of the power and security of the state. The loggietta, to the right of this picture, at the base of the campanile, was a small waiting chamber used by representatives of the various scuole. The doge and the executive councils of state came from the main door of the Doge's Palace, which is hidden from view around the corner of San Marco, and processed in a straight line to the loggietta, where they joined with members of the scuole. In this way, the procession not only marked out the hierarchical differences between the governing nobility and the citizens of Venice, but also emphasized the unity of all in the service of Venice.

Piazza San Marco: looking South-east

Painted c.1735–40
114 × 154 cm
National Gallery of Art, Washington, DC

A·C·F·

Dolo is a small village on the Brenta Canal, along which Canaletto travelled in 1740–1 with his nephew Bernardo Bellotto. In the foreground is a sluice-gate and in the middle of the canal, with a blue-and-white striped awning, we can see the *Burchiello* or ferry boat that transports travellers towards Padua. The scene depicted here is repeated in an etching published in 1744, though it has been noted that the style of this picture is more closely related to Canaletto's work of the 1720s, since there is no noteworthy architectural edifice and the scene seems more to relate to the happy passing of time on a warm summer afternoon than to be a sophisticated view for the Grand Tourist. The characters dotted around this composition are varied, as in Canaletto's early work, and not without interest. Workmen loaf about, a mother and child to the left confront a gaggle of geese, while a small group of well-heeled travellers are either waiting for the Burchiello or are discussing what to do next. This group is a brilliant dash of colour, which invigorates the whole composition, providing the viewer with both an anchor and a point of departure.

Dolo on the Brenta

Painted 1730s or 1741–42
80 × 95.3 cm
Staatsgalerie, Stuttgart

In 1742 Canaletto took the hitherto unknown step of signing and dating five pictures of Rome. These were commissioned by Joseph Smith at a time when Canaletto had little other work. The downturn in Canaletto's trade was partly caused by a decline in the numbers of Grand Tourists coming to Venice and quite possibly because he had become stale from painting Venice without a break for fifteen years. It seems clear that Canaletto did not go to Rome in order to paint these pictures but relied on drawings he had made in 1719–20 on his last visits to the 'Eternal City'. The considerable size of these canvases suggests that Joseph Smith intended them as part of the decorative scheme, perhaps for his palazzo on the Grand Canal.

In this picture we see Grand Tourists, standing on the Via Sacra (Sacred Way), learning about the Roman Forum. The young lords in coloured tunics converse with dour tutors dressed in black and wearing short powdered wigs. They are admiring the three remaining columns of the Temple of Castor and Pollux on the Sacred Way, which leads past the Temple of Saturn, towards the Capitoline Hill. The pagan temples of Jupiter and Juno that once stood there had long since been cleared away to be replaced by the Senate House, above which a tower rises surmounted by Christ in Benediction.

Rome: Ruins of the Forum, looking Towards the Capitol

Painted 1742

188 × 104 cm

Royal Collection

ANT·CANAL. FECIT
ANNO MCCXLII

The Pantheon is arguably the greatest building in Rome. The scale of its dimensions and the harmony of its interior have caused wonder throughout the centuries, and no résumé of the ancient world would be complete without it. Built by the Emperor Hadrian, it replaced a pre-existing temple constructed by M. Agrippa, as is noted in the inscription on the portico. It was a temple for all the gods and was subsequently turned into a church. During the pontificate of Urban VIII (1624–48), the two towers by Bernini were added above the portico, and the bronze casing of the interior was removed to make the baldacchino above the relics of St Peter in the Vatican. Grand Tourists of the eighteenth century who were blessed with good fortune could visit the Pantheon in times of flood by boat and view its huge cavernous space by the light of candles and the moon shining through the great oculus at the top of the dome.

In comparison with other paintings by Canaletto, the composition of this picture is unimaginative and the figures rather flat and lifeless. The proportions of the Pantheon, the square in front of it and the vistas leading from it are all good fodder for a dynamic, exciting composition, and yet in this picture the Pantheon is made to look squat and dumpy.

Even though it is generally accepted that Joseph Smith commissioned this picture, doubts have been expressed over its authenticity on grounds of quality. An explanation might be that Canaletto had not seen the Pantheon since 1719–20, and that amongst the drawings we know he made while in Rome in his youth there is no view of the building, though there are views of the three other subjects he painted for Smith. It seems likely therefore that Canaletto borrowed drawings or engravings, perhaps from Bernardo Bellotto, as a source for this picture.

Rome: the Pantheon

Painted 1742
183.2 × 105.4 cm
Royal Collection

M. AGRIPPA L. F. COS. TERTIVM FECIT
ANT. CANAL FECIT
ANNO MDCCXLII

Of all Canaletto's capricci this is one of his best and most erudite jokes. Andrea Palladio submitted designs for the Rialto Bridge when it was in dire need of replacement. Canaletto knew of Palladio's design from his *I quattro libri dell'architettura*, which was published in 1570. The following is an extract from Palladio's description of his own bridge:

The river is very broad, and the bridge would have been in the very spot where the merchants assemble to treat of their affairs. Therefore to keep up the said grandeur and dignity of the said city and also to add a very great income to it, I have upon the bridge, in its full breadth, three streets . . . On each side of these streets, I have ordered shops so that there would have been six rows of them.

In addition, Palladio planned great loggias at either end of the bridge to provide meeting space for traders, an idea drawn from the bridge of Aelius in Rome. Though conspicuous in design and so appropriate to the grandeur of Venice, as well as commercially promising in terms of shop leases, the design was ultimately flawed because the piers for the three arches would have obstructed water traffic.

Capriccio: a Palladian Design for the Rialto Bridge

Painted 1742
90 × 130 cm
Royal Collection

At the bottom of the nearest plinth to the viewer is a well-dressed man who is looking justly intrigued by what he sees. He is studying the four horses of San Marco, which were brought to Venice after the Fourth Crusade in 1204. They were thought to have adorned the great Hippodrome in Istanbul and were long considered to be fragments from the Greek world. They were known to have been placed on the loggia of San Marco by the middle of the thirteenth century and always remained there until Napoleon carried them off to Paris in 1797. The man's confusion is entirely justified, because Canaletto has fashioned another capriccio by moving the horses from their celebrated position on to monumental plinths in the Piazzetta.

For art historians, Canaletto has left another riddle. Again on the nearest plinth, there is a date inscribed MCCCXXXII or 1332, which is especially confusing because it is clear that this picture was one of thirteen capricci commissioned by Joseph Smith in 1743. If, however, 1332 refers to the number of years after the foundation of Venice in 421, the calculation is wrong by only ten years, with one X too many in the inscription. This idea is supported by the inscription at the bottom of the plinth which refers to Pietro Grimani, who was doge from 1741 to 1752. This would satisfy the assumed date of the picture as 1743 and exclude the implied date of 1753.

Capriccio: the Horses of San Marco in the Piazzetta

Painted 1743

103 × 129.5 cm

Royal Collection

The Molo: looking West with the Doge's Palace and the Prison

Painted 1743
50.5 × 95.5 cm
Royal Collection

This picture, signed and dated 24 October 1743, is in the smaller format produced for the Grand Tourist trade. However, it became part of the Smith Collection after it had been engraved by Visentini, together with other views of the Piazzetta, ready for publication by Smith's own publishing house, Pasquali. Such a publication was probably a ploy to counter competition from Michele Marieschi, who in 1741 had published his own engraved views of Venice, and thus challenged Canaletto's position as the principal topographical illustrator of the city.

In common with many views by Canaletto of the late 1730s, this picture is somewhat perfunctory in execution in the sense that the paint is thin and flat, lacking the vigour and loose impasto of his earlier work in Venice. Additionally, there is much evident use of the ruler and the figures are puppets on a stage rather than the lively cosmopolitan inhabitants of Venice he had once painted.

In spite of its shortcomings, the painting is a remarkable and comprehensive view of the principal buildings of state as they lie along the Molo. Nearest to us is the Prison, followed by the Doge's Palace. Behind it is the campanile, which should be further to the right, and across the Piazzetta, past the columns of St Mark and St Theodore, we see the Library with its Roman Ionic proportions. This style of architecture was brought to Venice by Sansovino following the Sack of Rome in 1527, and the same architect was responsible for the design of the State Mint, which is the white building just beyond the Library. Finally, it is possible to see the orange building of the grain market to the far left.

With the Basilica of San Marco beyond the Doge's Palace, this ensemble of buildings formed the nerve centre of a large empire, representing perhaps the most compact collection of civic buildings ever planned in a European city.

Entrance to the Grand Canal: looking East

Painted 1744
127 × 203 cm
Royal Collection

The years 1741–46 are generally known as a period of diversification for Canaletto; a time in which he explored etching as a new medium, painted in Rome for the first time and invented many engaging capricci. His paintings of Venice from this period are not often of an exceptional standard, with little of his once-legendary luminous light and languid figures. This painting of Santa Maria della Salute and the entrance to the Grand Canal is remarkable, however, for its daring composition and a searing quality of light, which recalls Canaletto's work for Stefano Conti twenty years before.

This picture is painted on the very large scale at which Canaletto usually excelled. The size of the canvas and the resultant difficulties of moving it suggest that it was perhaps for the home market, and its subsequent ownership by Joseph Smith hints that it was commissioned by Canaletto's great patron.

As with so many of Canaletto's paintings, the underlying satisfaction of the picture lies with the pleasing composition, to which the artist was prepared to sacrifice much in his view. Who else would so savagely edit the church of Santa Maria della Salute in order to maintain a neat triangular arrangement between the side of the dome, the top of the pediment, through the distant weathercock to the edge of the steps? Thus the Salute dominates the right-hand side while being linked by the above triangle to the middle of the picture.

Canaletto makes the view more cosy by shrouding the foreground in cold shadow while illuminating the middle ground with an appealing shaft of southern sunlight. This and other features, such as the invigorating sky and the use of red flashes to lead the spectator's eye around the composition are familiar techniques seemingly borrowed from Canaletto's early career.

The church of Santa Maria della Salute, designed by Baldassare Longhena, was one of the few seventeenth-century buildings in Venice. It represented a spectacular architectural celebration of her redemption from the 1630 plague. Disease was a common occurrence and a preoccupying fear for Venetians, for they had no independent fresh-water supply and even the most vigilant customs officers could not protect the city from infection from the trading fleets. The relief felt by the city is perhaps illustrated by the lengths to which the builders went in order to erect this great edifice: there are 1,700,000 piles underneath this church, forming a secure base for the foundations.

Beyond the Salute one can see a ball supported by two figures surmounted by a man acting as a wind vane. It is from this point Canaletto imagined the view *The Bacino di San Marco Looking East* (page 73).

Of all the views of the Thames by Canaletto, this is perhaps the most imaginative. The view we see here is of the City of London, bracketed by the centring of one of the arches of Westminster Bridge. The centring was the wooden structure which formed a mask upon which the dressed stone of the arch was positioned, until the final stabilizing keystone was placed here in July 1746, shortly after Canaletto's arrival in London. As if to emphasize the fact that this was a building site, Canaletto put in a fair amount of tackle and rope, as well as an idle bucket.

To the far left of the cityscape we see a wooden water-tower and the York Water Gate from which spot Canaletto had made a drawing (see page 32). Various spires show against the skyline – St Clement Danes, St Bride's and the dome of St Paul's Cathedral.

The contemporary significance of Westminster Bridge cannot be underestimated, for with it lay the key to the development of the South Bank. Many fought against its construction, arguing that the water level would be raised by three feet, and the Wardens of St Thomas's Hospital feared that five thousand would drown in a sudden deluge. Despite opposition, a Bridge Committee was formed in 1736. On this committee sat both the Duke of Richmond and Sir Hugh Smithson (later the Duke of Northumberland), both of whom played significant parts in Canaletto's English career. The first stone of the bridge was eventually sunk in 1739.

London seen through an Arch of Westminster Bridge

Painted c.1746

57 × 95 cm

The Duke of Northumberland

This painting shows the Lord Mayor's Day celebrations on 29 October 1746. The new mayor of London is taking a barge from the City upstream to Westminster Hall to be sworn into office. Canaletto shows the Thames teeming with life and colour, capturing the full pageantry of the occasion. Boats and ships fire salutes to the mayor while his City barge in the centre foreground is accompanied by barges from the City of London guilds. From right to left, the guilds represented are the Drapers, the Mercers, the Fishmongers, the Goldsmiths and the Skinners; while in the distance under the bridge are the barges of the Goldworkers, Vintners and the Merchant Taylors guilds. On the banks of the Thames, we see the ribbon development to the south towards Lambeth Palace, the seat of the Bishop of London. On the north bank we can see the old arrangement of government buildings before the 1834 fire which necessitated the rebuilding of the Palace of Westminster. We can clearly see Westminster Abbey, Westminster Hall, and the churches St Stephen's, St Margaret's and St John the Evangelist at Smith Square.

The contemporary significance of Westminster Bridge has already been discussed, and the reader might be amused to note that Canaletto anticipated wrongly the final appearance of the bridge. The painting dates from 1746, but the bridge was not finally finished until 1750 and, although Canaletto has included the planned central statutes of Thames and Isis in good faith, these were never actually executed.

In 1747, this picture was engraved by Remigius Parr and published by John Brindley. As if to emphasize the commercial aspect of this scheme, the engraved version includes the barge of the Stationers' Guild, perhaps to secure some sales from that market. There are several similar bird's-eye views of the Thames, which suggests that Canaletto had struck on the right topical subject in order to secure his reputation, having just arrived in London.

London: Westminster Bridge from the North on Lord Mayor's Day

Painted 1746

96 × 137.5 cm

Yale Center for British Art, New Haven. Paul Mellon Collection

Joseph Smith gave a letter of introduction to Canaletto, which was addressed to Owen McSwiney. The target for a commission was Charles Lennox, the second Duke of Richmond. The ploy worked and it is assumed that in 1747 Canaletto began work on the drawings for this illustrated view of the Thames from Richmond House. To the left is the house of the second Duke of Montagu, and on the terrace are members of the Richmond family enjoying the midday sun.

For the improvement of the composition, Canaletto has brought the Thames closer on both the south side and the curve of the north bank, thus bringing into sharp focus Old Somerset House, which at the time was the Royal Dower House. Shining out from the skyline is St Paul's Cathedral, finished only twenty-six years before, ranged with the recently constructed church spires of Wren and Hawksmoor. The Lord Mayor's barge and another barge are being rowed down the middle of the river, surrounded by waterboatmen ferrying their fares across the River Thames. It was these waterboatmen who so savagely attacked the plans for a bridge at Westminster, and looking at this image of bliss, who can blame them?

The texture of Canaletto's paint is thin and reveals the underpaint, which has been applied in a series of blobs. It was this aspect of Canaletto's style that George Vertue was to question in his criticism of Canaletto in 1749.

London: the Thames and City of London from Richmond House

Painted 1747

105 × 117 cm

The Goodwood Trustees, Goodwood

The procession of the Knights of the Order of the Bath was one of the few ceremonial pictures that Canaletto painted while in England. The Dean of Westminster, Joseph Wilcocks, commissioned this painting to celebrate the installation of the Knights of this Order on 20 June 1749. The Order of the Bath was re-established by King George I as a body of thirty-six companions. The name 'Bath' stems from the bathing ceremony that formed the principal rite of admission to the original Order, thought to have been formed on the coronation of Henry IV in 1399.

This is a particularly interesting view of London because it illustrates the new west end of Westminster Abbey completed in 1745, and an area of Westminster which changed so radically after the fire at the Palace of Westminster in 1834, which led to the subsequent building of the current Houses of Parliament and the clock tower. Though the painting is topographically interesting, Canaletto has sadly failed to depict a real, vivid and colourful scene.

London: Westminster Abbey with a Procession of the Knights of the Bath

Painted 1749

99 × 101.5 cm

Dean and Chapter of Westminster

This is a view of the east wall of Warwick Castle. The pendant for this picture shows the other side of the wall from the courtyard, and is one of five portraits painted of the house and estate of Lord Brooke, at Warwick. It is clear that the castle views were painted both before and after Canaletto's visit to Venice and that the illustrated picture could date from either period. Throughout, however, we can be sure that Canaletto was paid around £30 for each of his paintings.

Since 1068 there has been a castle at Warwick, originally built by the Normans to dominate a town which has often held a significant place in English history. Strategically located on the principal road to the north, Warwick was also the seat of Richard Neville, the power-broker and king-maker of the Wars of the Roses.

The east front pictured by Canaletto was known by Neville, and is part of a substantial redevelopment of the original fortress by two generations of the Beauchamp family between 1325 and 1359. To the left is the impressive Caesar's Tower with its two-tier fortifications and elaborate stonework, which in keeping with the rest of the façade, seems conspicuously flamboyant rather than defensive. In the mid-eighteenth century, Lord Brooke sought advice from the landscape gardener 'Capability' Brown, who planted many trees, made new walkways and generally softened the lines of the castle.

Lord Brooke's interest in the building is certainly reflected in the many commemorative pictures he commissioned. Equally, a changed view of the castle is clearly illustrated by the way in which Canaletto has depicted the building as an Arcadian backdrop to the pursuit of leisure and idle, though no doubt sophisticated discourse.

Warwick Castle: the East Front

Painted 1748–49

73 × 122 cm

Birmingham City Museum and Art Gallery

London: Greenwich Hospital from the North Bank of the Thames

Painted c.1753

66 × 112.5 cm

National Maritime Museum, Greenwich

In common with other pictures from Canaletto's English period, this is clearly a portrait of a specific building. However, unlike the portraits of Alnwick or Warwick Castles, this was probably not painted at the behest of a particular patron but as a speculative view of a topical building which, after decades of construction and almost a century of thought, was all but complete.

Building on the site began with The Queen's House, which lies in the distance between the two cupolas of the Hospital. Originally built by Inigo Jones for Henrietta Maria, wife of Charles I, it remained unsold after the latter's execution and finally reverted to Charles II at the restoration of the monarchy in 1660. Charles commissioned new gardens, using the services of Lenôtre who had worked at Versailles for Louis XIV, and established the Royal Observatory behind The Queen's House on the hill. French taste and sensibility were foremost in late seventeenth- and early eighteenth-century Europe, and the inauguration of Les Invalides by Louis XIV encouraged William and Mary and subsequent monarchs to finance both Chelsea Hospital, for infantry, and the Greenwich Hospital, for seamen, as laudable, philanthropic and kingly acts of generosity.

The culmination of this great scheme coincides with Canaletto's known activity around 1753–4, when he was working for Thomas Hollis. It seems plausible, therefore, in the absence of any other information, that this painting can be ascribed to the later years of Canaletto's time in England.

Alnwick Castle, one of the seats of the Percy family, was owned by Sir Hugh Smithson, later the Duke of Northumberland. Smithson proved to be one of Canaletto's most reliable patrons and, after Canaletto's return from Venice in 1751, he commissioned a view of Northumberland House in London and another of Alnwick Castle in Northumberland.

Looking at the evocative shapes created by the castle walls and its keep, it is slightly surprising that Canaletto did not make a more imaginative composition out of this subject. It has been suggested that he never visited Alnwick, which would have involved at least nine days of uncomfortable travel from London, and that consequently he had to rely on existing watercolours and engravings by artists of a lesser calibre. If this is so, it is not surprising that there are several uncharacteristic failings in this painting. In particular, the figures dotted around the landscape seem rather flat, and in some areas their scale, in proportion to their position, can be misleading.

Alnwick Castle, Northumberland

Painted 1752
113.5 × 139.5 cm
The Duke of Northumberland

This picture of Old Walton Bridge was commissioned by Thomas Hollis, who was in regular correspôndence with Joseph Smith, in Venice. Perhaps encouraged by Smith, Hollis commissioned six pictures from Canaletto, which vary considerably in subject and cannot be described as a set. Each picture is, however, inscribed and dated 1754.

The wooden latticed bridge spanning the Thames at Walton in Middlesex, was paid for by Samuel Dicker, MP for Plymouth, whose house is shown on the left-hand side of the opposite bank amongst the trees. Dicker subsequently owned a similar picture upon which Canaletto also noted that it was unique. Within the oeuvre of Canaletto, this picture for Hollis is both a rare and charming landscape. The sky is full of drifting English cumulus cloud, the greens are deep and the foliage lush, and for the first time Canaletto appears to have painted an English landscape in an English way. Also for the first time, Canaletto may have included a portrait of the patron, who walks towards us from the party on the river bank.

Old Walton Bridge

Painted 1754
48.9 × 76.8 cm
Dulwich Picture Gallery, London

Ranelagh Gardens were at Chelsea, and when this entertainment park opened in 1742, it rivalled Vauxhall Gardens. The picture illustrated is of the Rotunda, a large meeting hall lined with boxes, which could accommodate six or seven hundred diners. It was built by William Jones in 1741 and was clearly based upon the Pantheon in Rome, with the addition of a large central column which acted both as a structural support and as an enormous fireplace. Even though its fortunes changed after the opening of Westminster Bridge and the increased accessibility of Vauxhall Gardens, it was still popular enough to be the venue for a Mozart concert in 1764. This picture, along with a series depicting Vauxhall Gardens, represents a change in Canaletto's work, following his return from Venice in 1754.

By painting views of public entertainment, Canaletto did not have to rely on the patronage of private patrons, but could sell to a much broader public. Most of these views were engraved and distributed to a wider market, in this case by N. Parr, or in the case of Vauxhall Gardens by Robert Sayer and Henry Overton.

London: Ranelagh, the Interior of the Rotunda

Painted 1754

46 × 75.5 cm

National Gallery, London

This painting shows Eton College, with its surrounding school buildings, the town, and the Thames in the foreground. The topography of the chapel and school are accurate, but the buildings to the left do not correspond with any known structures.

Canaletto had visited Windsor in 1747 to paint a view of Windsor Castle, which was commissioned by Sir Hugh Smithson, who later became the Duke of Northumberland. On the basis of style, however, this painting appears to date from the same period as the Hollis pictures, around 1754. If the painting was executed well after Canaletto's visit to the spot, the inaccuracies might be explained by a lapse of memory or muddled interpretation of earlier sketches. No documentation survives to inform us of the original patron although the painting was part of the collection of the Earls of Lovelace.

Eton College Chapel

Painted c.*1754*
61.5 × 107.5 cm
National Gallery, London

Capriccio with San Giorgio Maggiore and the Rialto Bridge

Painted c.*1746–55*

165 × 114.5 cm

North Carolina Museum of Art, Raleigh, NC

This capriccio is one of the more curious and imaginative of Canaletto's inventions. He has taken the façade of the Palladian church of San Giorgio Maggiore and placed it next to the Rialto Bridge, though in reality they are almost a kilometre apart. The choice of theme is reminiscent of the overdoors commissioned by Joseph Smith in 1743, of Palladian buildings in a Venetian cityscape. This painting, however, is almost two metres high, which suggests that it is part of a large wall decoration and that it was quite probably part of a set. The provenance of this picture is not known but the campanile of San Bartolomeo, rising behind the church of San Giorgio, was demolished in 1747, which suggests that the work was commissioned before Canaletto's departure for England, or that he painted it from memory for an English client. We know that Canaletto painted capricci in England and the lack of characteristic detail within this picture may support the idea of English patronage.

San Giorgio Maggiore was the Benedictine church in Venice, and as such one of the most cherished in the city. According to the preference of Benedictines for isolation, the church and monastery of San Giorgio are on an island in the lagoon and they can be clearly seen in Canaletto's large picture of the corner of the Doge's Palace and the column of San Marco, commissioned by Joseph Smith *c.*1727 (page 67). This capriccio is made more curious because it is the only close view of San Giorgio, in spite of the fame and popularity of the church within the city and with visiting tourists. Canaletto perhaps did not paint it before because its island location presented too many compositional problems.

The varied and improbable landscape of this picture makes it one of the more extraordinary works by Canaletto in his English period. The countryside looks both English and Italian at the same time, with the lush greenery of the north and the craggy dry rocks of the south.

The architectural elements also have an international flavour. The Corinthian column in the foreground carries a coat of arms and a Venetian-style escutcheon. At some distance to the left is a Roman arch, to the right of which is a campanile, very like the one at San Pietro di Castello in Venice. In the middle distance, we can see the familiar looping arches of Westminster Bridge set in a contemporary English landscape, and in the far distance the prickly skyline of London. In creating his ideal and architecturally delicious world, Canaletto has cleverly provided two vanishing points which recede diagonally into the depths of the picture.

This is one of two capricci known as 'The Lovelace Capriccios', thought to have been commissioned by Lord King, whose descendant, the Earl of Lovelace, sold them fifty years ago. Fortunately for us, however, one of these pictures is initialled and dated 1754 by Canaletto.

Capriccio: River Landscape with a Column and a Ruined Roman Arch and Reminiscences of England

Painted 1754

132 × 106.5 cm

National Gallery of Art, Washington, DC

San Marco: the Interior

Painted c.*1755*
36.5 × 33.5 cm
Royal Collection

Views of interiors are particularly rare in Canaletto's work, and this small cabinet painting is one of two which he painted inside San Marco. Both views were sold to George III from Joseph Smith's collection in 1762. The first picture dates from the late 1720s, and the view illustrated here was executed between Canaletto's return from England in 1755 and the eventual sale to the King in 1762.

The scene depicts midday Mass as the sun shines through the great south window of San Marco, glancing off golden mosaics and illuminating the choirs in their raised choir stalls. Those attending church are from all walks of life and are wearing sober daytime clothes, while two dogs play in the foreground.

There are, however, some inconsistencies. For example, the lancet windows in the domes issue no light, which is surprising given the time of day and the amount of light flooding the south transept. Also, the heavy coats of arms representing different doges which hang from the nave balcony were prohibited from the early 1720s for reasons of structural safety. This does not mean to say, however, that they were not brought out for special occasions.

Night Festival at San Pietro di Castello

Painted before 1763
119 × 187 cm
Gemäldegalerie, Berlin.

For a painter to paint at night is almost a contradiction in terms, and this picture of San Pietro di Castello is truly exceptional in Canaletto's work. It was commissioned by Sigismund Streit, a German trader from Berlin who arrived in Venice in 1709. He stayed, became rich as a merchant and retired to live at Padua from 1754 until his death in 1775. In 1763 he presented his considerable collection of pictures to his old school in Berlin, the Gymnasium zum Grauen Kloster. This later date is the only real clue to the date of this picture, but it is generally assumed that Canaletto painted this, and three other pictures, between his return from England and the year of the gift, 1763. The elegant Palladian design of San Pietro and its towering campanile, the top of which was designed by Mauro Coducci, shrouds the ancient heritage of the site. San Pietro had once been the residence of the patriarch of Venice and until 1807 this church was the cathedral of Venice. Set on the far north-eastern edge of the city, it is a remote place and was rarely visited by Grand Tourists, but for a resident who knew the city well, the festival at San Pietro on 28 June, the eve of the feast day of St Peter and St Paul, would have been significant.

A quotation from William Beckford perhaps gives some idea of the scene even though he was writing about the Grand Canal:

As night approached, innumerable tapers glimmered through the awnings before the windows. Every boat had its lantern, and the gondolas, moving rapidly along, were followed by tracts of light, which gleamed and played in the waters.

Capriccio: a Colonnade Opening onto the Courtyard of a Palace

Painted 1765
131 × 93 cm
Accademia, Venice

In September 1763, Canaletto was finally elected as a member of the Accademia di Belle Arti (Academy of Fine Arts) in Venice. This picture was his presentation piece, which was accepted in 1765.

It may at first seem strange that the Accademia, formed in 1757, had not elected Canaletto before 1763, but when it is considered that topographical painting was low on the scale of creativity it becomes clear that no amount of fame would place Canaletto above even the most lowly figure painter. It is interesting to note that in his presentation picture Canaletto goes almost as far as it is possible to be 'creative' without ceasing to be a topographical painter. The building, for example, is loosely based on the Ca' d'Oro, the most famous Gothic palace in Venice, but most of the architectural detailing has been classicized. There is no limit to the vista and the areas of space which Canaletto invents. He opens great thermal windows in the ceiling of the colonnade to create a nonsensical barrel vault every two bays.

Totally contrived and tirelessly absorbing, this picture is reminiscent of Giovanni Battista Piranesi's etchings, *Carceri d'invenzione* (Imaginary Prisons), published in 1745. As usual, Canaletto has broken up the scene with figures, at compositionally strategic points, but these people do not have the animated charm of his early work. They all seem self-absorbed and almost chilling, as the kneeling figure, possibly a beggar, stares out at us.

This picture was highly acclaimed by contemporaries and it was much copied. There is something ironic in the thought that Canaletto's fame in England was based on his realistic depictions of nature, and that it was only close to his death that he became a local hero in Venice, on the basis of his inventions.

CHRONOLOGY

1674
Possible birth of Joseph Smith.
1697
28 October – Birth of Giovanni Antonio Canal (Canaletto).
1703
Publication of Carlevaris's etchings, *Le Fabriche e Vedute di Venezia*.
1719–20
Visits Rome with his father to design scenery for *Tito Sempronio Gracco* and *Turno Aricino*.
1720
Birth of Bernardo Bellotto.
1723
Possible Liechtenstein commission.
Piazza San Marco repaving started.
1725
Through Alessandro Marchesini, Stefano Conti commissions two paintings by Canaletto.
1726
Participates in two paintings of imaginary tombs commissioned by Owen McSwiney.
1727
McSwiney documents the completion of two copper plates for the Duke of Richmond.
1730
Joseph Smith orders two paintings by Canaletto for Samuel Hill.
Death of Carlevaris.
1735
Publication of the first edition of *Prospectus Magni Canalis Venetiarum*.
1738
Bellotto becomes a member of the painters' guild, the Fraglia.
1739
Building work begun on Westminster Bridge.
1740–41
Journeys up the Brenta Canal with Bellotto.
1741
War of Austrian Succession.
1742
Signs five large views of Rome.
Bellotto signs etchings 'B.B. detto Canaleto fe'.
Publication of the second edition of *Prospectus*.
1743
Francesco Algarotti in Venice.
1744
Joseph Smith appointed British Consul.
Publication of a series of etchings produced for Joseph Smith.

1746
Arrival in London.
Commissioned to paint Richmond House.
Paints the celebrations on Lord Mayor's Day.
1747
Completes the painting of Windsor Castle for Sir Hugh Smithson.
Bellotto leaves Venice to become court painter to the Elector of Saxony.
1748
First payment from Lord Brooke is received for his paintings of Warwick Castle: £58.
1749
Lord Brooke pays Canaletto £31 10s.
One arch of Westminster Bridge is dismantled and repair begun.
Starts to paint Syon House, reported by Sir Hugh Smithson.
Paints the procession of the Knights of the Bath at Westminster Abbey.
Invites the public to view a painting at his house to refute rumours that he is not the real Canaletto.
1750
Returns to Venice.
1751
Invests the sum of 2,150 ducats in the lease on a property on the Zattere, Venice.
Third edition of *Prospectus* is published.
Returns to England and issues a second invitation to the public to visit his studio.
Commissioned to paint a portrait of Northumberland House.
1752
Record of further payments made by Lord Brooke to Canaletto for £33 12s and £30 respectively.
1753
Possible short visit to Venice.
1754
Inscribes and dates four pictures for Thomas Hollis.
Dates a capriccio, later to belong to Lord Lovelace.
Paints a view of the Rotunda at Ranelagh.
1755
Inscribes and dates *Old Walton Bridge* for Samuel Dicker.
Returns to Venice.
1760
Meets John Crewe and Edward Hinchcliffe, selling to them his painting of Whitehall and the Privy Garden.
Smith retires from being Consul.
1762
Smith sells fifty Canalettos to George III.

1763
Is elected to join the Accademia di Belle Arti, Venice.
1765
Signs and dates his capriccio presentation piece for the Accademia.
1768
Death of Canaletto.
1770
Death of Joseph Smith.
1780
Death of Bernardo Bellotto.
1797
Venice falls at the hands of Napoleon.

SOURCES AND ACKNOWLEDGEMENTS

The principal sources used for this book have been W.G. CONSTABLE's fully illustrated *Catalogue raisonné* of Canaletto, which was later revised by J.G. LINKS (Oxford, 1976), and J.G. LINKS' own invaluable works; *Canaletto and His Patrons* (London and New York, 1977) and *Canaletto* (Oxford, 1982). Other works referred to, though to a lesser degree, are listed below. Lastly, my thanks to Rosemary and Robert Woodward for allowing me to illustrate from their private collection, to Sarah Baldwin, Sarah Carr-Gomm, Tom Parsons and the editorial staff of Studio Editions.

BIBLIOGRAPHY

KATHERINE BAETJER AND J.G. LINKS, *Canaletto*, Exhibition catalogue, The Metropolitan Museum of Art, 1989.
RUTH BROMBERG, *Canaletto's Etchings*, London, 1974.
HILDA F. FINBERG, 'Canaletto and his Patrons', *Walpole Society Journal*, 1920–1.
FRANCIS HASKELL, *Patrons and Painters*, London and New Haven, 1980.
FRANCIS HASKELL, 'Stefano Conti, Patron of Canaletto and Others', *Burlington Magazine*, 98, September 1956.
CHRISTOPHER HIBBERT, *The Grand Tour*, London, 1987.
CHRISTOPHER HIBBERT, *Venice, The Biography of a City*, London, 1988.
MICHAEL LEVEY, *The Later Italian Pictures in the Collection of H.M. The Queen*, London, 1964.
SIR OLIVER MILLAR, *Canaletto, Paintings and Drawings*, Exhibition catalogue, The Queen's Gallery Buckingham Palace, 1981–2.
GIANCARLO VILLA, *An Introduction to Venice*, Venice, 1983.

LIST OF PLATES

All works are by Canaletto unless otherwise stated

51 *The Grand Canal: Rialto Bridge from the North*, 1725. Oil on canvas, 91.5 × 134.5 cm. Private collection. Photo: The Art Gallery of Ontario.

53 *The Grand Canal: looking North from near the Rialto Bridge*, 1725. Oil on canvas, 90 × 132 cm. Private collection. Photo: The Art Gallery of Ontario.

55 *The Grand Canal: from Santa Maria della Carità to the Bacino di San Marco*, 1726. Oil on canvas, 90 × 132 cm. Private collection. Photo: The Art Gallery of Ontario.

57 *Santi Giovanni e Paolo and the Scuola di San Marco*, 1725. Oil on canvas, 125 × 165 cm. Gemaldegalerie Alte Meister, Staatliche Kunstsammlungen, Dresden.

59 *San Giacomo di Rialto*, c.1725–30. Oil on canvas, 95.5 × 117 cm. Gemaldegalerie Alte Meister, Staatliche Kunstsammlungen, Dresden.

61 *Entrance to the Grand Canal: from the Piazzetta*, c.1727. Oil on canvas, 170 × 135.5 cm. Royal Collection, St James's Palace © Her Majesty the Queen.

63 *Piazzetta San Marco: looking West from the North End of the Piazzetta*, c.1727. Oil on canvas, 170 × 129.3 cm. Royal Collection, St James's Palace © Her Majesty the Queen.

65 *The Piazzetta: looking North*, c.1727. Oil on canvas, 170.2 × 129.5 cm. Royal Collection, St James's Palace © Her Majesty the Queen.

67 *Piazzetta: looking South*, c.1727. Oil on canvas, 170.2 × 132 cm. Royal Collection, St James's Palace © Her Majesty the Queen.

69 *The Grand Canal: Rialto Bridge from the South*, 1727. Oil on copper, 45.5 × 62.5 cm. Viscount Coke, Holkham Hall, Norfolk.

71 *The Grand Canal: 'The Stonemason's Yard'*, c.1728. Oil on canvas, 124 × 163 cm. National Gallery, London.

73 *The Bacino di San Marco: looking East*, c.1726–38. Oil on canvas, 124.5 × 204.5 cm. Museum of Fine Arts, Boston. Abbot Lawrence Fund, Seth K. Sweetser Fund and Charles Edward French Fund.

75 *Piazza San Marco: looking North*, c.1729. Oil on canvas, 53 × 70.5 cm. The Nelson-Atkins Museum of Art, Kansas City, Missouri (Nelson Fund) 55–36.

77 *Riva degli Schiavoni: looking East*, c.1730. Oil on copper, 26 × 62 cm. Devonshire Collection Trustees, Chatsworth.

79 *San Marco: an Evening Service*, c.1730. Oil on canvas, 28.6 × 19.7 cm. Royal Collection, St James's Palace © Her Majesty the Queen.

81 *San Christoforo, San Michele and Murano: from Fondamenta Nuova*, 1725–30. Oil on canvas, 142.2 × 150.5 cm. Dallas Museum of Art.

83 *A Puppet Show on the Piazzetta*, c.1725–30. Oil on canvas, 24 × 31 cm. The Ashmolean Museum, Oxford.

85 *The Arsenale: the Water Entrance*, c.1732. Oil on canvas, 46 × 78.8 cm. Woburn Abbey: reproduced by kind permission of the Marquess of Tavistock and the Trustees of the Bedford Estate.

87 *A Regatta on the Grand Canal*, c.1733. Oil on canvas, 77 × 126 cm. Royal Collection, St James's Palace © Her Majesty the Queen.

89 *The Bacino di San Marco on Ascension Day*, 1732. Oil on canvas, 77 × 125 cm. Royal Collection, St James's Palace © Her Majesty the Queen.

91 *Santi Giovanni e Paolo and the Monument of Bartolomeo Colleoni*, 1735. Oil on canvas, 46 × 78 cm. Royal Collection, St James's Palace, © Her Majesty the Queen.

93 *The Doge visiting the Church and Scuola di San Rocco*, c.1735. Oil on canvas, 147 × 199 cm. National Gallery, London.

95 *Piazza San Marco: looking South-east*, c.1735–40. Oil on canvas, 114 × 154 cm. National Gallery of Art, Washington, DC. Gift of Mrs Barbara Hutton.

97 *Dolo on the Brenta*, 1730s or 1741–42. Oil on canvas, 80 × 95.3 cm. Staatsgalerie, Stuttgart.

99 *Rome: Ruins of the Forum: looking Towards the Capitol*, 1742. Oil on canvas, 188 × 104 cm. Royal Collection, St James's Palace © Her Majesty the Queen.

101 *Rome: the Pantheon*, 1742. Oil on canvas, 183.2 × 105.4 cm. Royal Collection, St James's Palace © Her Majesty the Queen.

103 *Capriccio: a Palladian Design for the Rialto Bridge*, 1742. Oil on canvas, 90 × 130 cm. Royal Collection, St James's Palace © Her Majesty the Queen.

105 *Capriccio: the Horses of San Marco in the Piazzetta*, 1743. Oil on canvas, 103 × 129.5 cm. Royal Collection, St James's Palace © Her Majesty the Queen.

107 *The Molo: looking West with the Doge's Palace and the Prison*, 1743. Oil on canvas, 50.5 × 95.5 cm. Royal Collection, St James's Palace © Her Majesty the Queen.

109 *Entrance to the Grand Canal: looking East*, 1744. Oil on canvas, 127 × 203 cm. Royal Collection, St James's Palace © Her Majesty the Queen.

111 *London seen through an Arch of Westminster Bridge*, c.1746. Oil on canvas, 57 × 95 cm. The Duke of Northumberland.

113 *London: Westminster Bridge from the North on Lord Mayor's Day*, 1746. Oil on canvas, 96 × 137.5 cm. Yale Center for British Art, New Haven. Paul Mellon Collection.

115 *London: the Thames and City of London from Richmond House*, 1747. Oil on canvas, 105 × 117 cm. The Goodwood Trustees, Goodwood.

117 *London: Westminster Abbey with a Procession of the Knights of the Bath*, 1749. Oil on canvas, 99 × 101.5 cm. Dean and Chapter of Westminster.

119 *Warwick Castle: the East Front*, 1748–49. Oil on canvas, 73 × 122 cm. Birmingham City Museum and Art Gallery.

121 *London: Greenwich Hospital from the North Bank of the Thames*, c.1753. Oil on canvas, 66 × 112.5 cm. National Maritime Museum, Greenwich.

123 *Alnwick Castle, Northumberland*, 1752. Oil on canvas, 113.5 × 139.5 cm. The Duke of Northumberland.

125 *Old Walton Bridge*, 1754. Oil on canvas, 48.9 × 76.8 cm. Dulwich Picture Gallery, London. By permission of the Governors of Dulwich College.

127 *London: Ranelagh, the Interior of the Rotunda*, 1754. Oil on canvas, 46 × 75.5 cm. National Gallery, London.

129 *Eton College Chapel*, c.1754. Oil on canvas, 61.5 × 107.5 cm. National Gallery, London.

131 *Capriccio with San Giorgio Maggiore and the Rialto Bridge*, c.1746–55. Oil on canvas, 165 × 114.5 cm. North Carolina Museum of Art, Raleigh, NC. Purchased with funds from the State of North Carolina.

133 *Capriccio: River Landscape with a Column and a Ruined Roman Arch and Reminiscences of England*, 1754. Oil on canvas, 132 × 106.5 cm. National Gallery of Art, Washington, DC. Paul Mellon Collection.

135 *San Marco: the Interior*, c.1755. Oil on canvas, 36.5 × 33.5 cm. Royal Collection, St James's Palace © Her Majesty the Queen.

137 *Night Festival at San Pietro di Castello*, before 1763. Oil on canvas, 119 × 187 cm. Gemaldegalerie, Berlin. Photo: Bildarchiv Preussicher Kulturbesitz.

139 *Capriccio: a Colonnade Opening onto the Courtyard of a Palace*, 1765. Oil on canvas, 131 × 93 cm. Accademia, Venice.